Cap de
Formentor

tor o

Fundación Yannick
Ben Jakober

anada

lcúdia

Parc Natural
de la Península
de Llevant

THE NORTHEAST

Artà   Capdepera   Cala Rajada

Serra de Llevant

*Coves
d'Artà*

Cala Millor

Punta de n'Amer

Porto
Cristo

*Coves del Drac
Coves dels Hams*

Serra de Llevant

D0892614

Cala d'Or

ural
ragó

TWINPACK GUIDE TO
Mallorca

How to Use This Book

KEY TO SYMBOLS

➕ Map reference to the accompanying fold-out map

✉ Address

☎ Telephone number

🕐 Opening/closing times

🍴 Restaurant or café

🚆 Nearest rail station

Ⓜ Nearest subway (Metro) station

🚌 Nearest bus route

🚢 Nearest riverboat or ferry stop

♿ Facilities for visitors with disabilities

❓ Other practical information

▷ Further information

ℹ Tourist information

✋ Admission charges:
Expensive (over €9),
Moderate (€3–€9) and
Inexpensive (under €3)

This guide is divided into the following sections

• Essential Mallorca: An introduction to the island and tips on making the most of your stay.

• Mallorca by Area: We've broken the island into five areas, and recommended the best sights, shops, activities, restaurants, entertainment and nightlife venues in each one. Suggested walks, a drive and a bike ride help you to explore.

• Where to Stay: The best hotels, whether you're looking for luxury, budget or something in between.

• Need to Know: The info you need to make your trip run smoothly, including getting about by public transport, weather tips, emergency phone numbers and useful websites.

Navigation In the Mallorca by Area chapter, we've given each area its own colour, which is also used on the locator maps throughout the book and the map on the inside front cover.

Maps The fold-out map accompanying this book is a comprehensive map of Mallorca. The grid on this fold-out map is the same as the grid on the locator maps within the book. The grid references to these maps are shown with capital letters, for example A1. The grid references to the town plan are shown with lower-case letters, for example a1.

Contents

Introducing Mallorca

Mallorca is what you make of it. The Mediterranean island delivers fantastic family beach holidays: the sea is clean and sunshine abundant. But if you want more from your break—art, food, history, sport—then Mallorca can spring more surprises.

The largest of the Balearic islands, Mallorca has long been a holiday destination for northern Europeans. Indeed, it has welcomed tourists since the 1920s and under Spain's General Franco it was the region's leading package-holiday destination. But in the last decade this beautiful island has shrugged off this weighty mantle; high-rise hotels have been replaced by sophisticated townhouse hotels and luxurious rural hotels. These days restaurant meals can delight the most discerning palates and the island's art galleries are known internationally. Majorca no more, modern Mallorca offers an amazingly well-balanced experience.

Of course, the reasons for the island's longevity as a holiday destination remain. With an alleged 300 days of sunshine—though the wise bring waterproofs in winter and spring—and sandy beaches, the island is perfect for a relaxing break. But there is such diversity of landscape and so many sights that it would be a shame to spend your holiday horizontal all the time. Vast, floodlit caverns with underground lakes? Check. Rugged mountain scenery with waymarked walks and overnight refuges? Check. Art ancient and modern? Check. Mallorca has survived a century of tourism and is set up to excel for another century.

However, many insiders say that it has taken outsiders and a younger Mallorcan generation to propel Mallorca forward. Many businesses are run by foreigners and the property market has long been dominated by Britons and Germans. That said, the authentic Mallorca, a pastoral paradise of almond and olive groves, isn't hard to find. Venture outside the resorts and you too will find much to fall in love with.

Facts + Figures

- **Population:** 869,067
- **Coastline:** 554km (343 miles)
- **Number of beaches:** 80
- **Number of caves:** 4,000
- **Number of spas:** 15
- **Number of tourists:** 9 million/year

ART AND LITERATURE

Mallorca's reputation for sun, sea and sand belies its strong artistic heritage. Not only have writers such as Robert Graves and Agatha Christie been inspired by the island, but painters and sculptors have left artworks from the miniature to the massive, such as Miquel Barceló's chapel in Palma's cathedral.

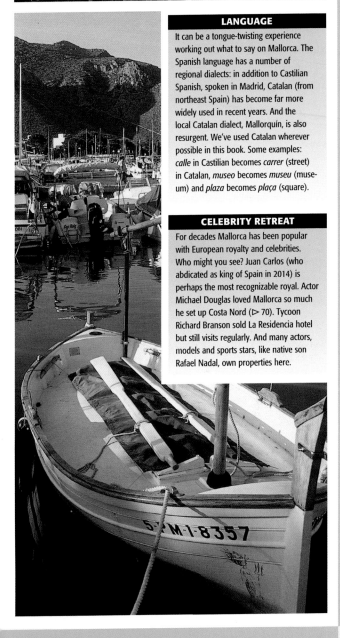

LANGUAGE

It can be a tongue-twisting experience working out what to say on Mallorca. The Spanish language has a number of regional dialects: in addition to Castilian Spanish, spoken in Madrid, Catalan (from northeast Spain) has become far more widely used in recent years. And the local Catalan dialect, Mallorquín, is also resurgent. We've used Catalan wherever possible in this book. Some examples: *calle* in Castilian becomes *carrer* (street) in Catalan, *museo* becomes *museu* (museum) and *plaza* becomes *plaça* (square).

CELEBRITY RETREAT

For decades Mallorca has been popular with European royalty and celebrities. Who might you see? Juan Carlos (who abdicated as king of Spain in 2014) is perhaps the most recognizable royal. Actor Michael Douglas loved Mallorca so much he set up Costa Nord (▷ 70). Tycoon Richard Branson sold La Residencia hotel but still visits regularly. And many actors, models and sports stars, like native son Rafael Nadal, own properties here.

A Short Stay in Mallorca

DAY 1: PALMA

Morning When staying at one of the hotels in the heart of Palma, if you don't have breakfast at your hotel, kickstart the day with an espresso at Bar Bosch, where Passeig des Born meets Carrer de la Unió. Spend the morning exploring the pedestrianized shopping streets of Palma's old town. There are big brands, boutiques and quirky shops selling anything from sweets to traditional *sobrassada* (spicy sausage).

Lunch Gradually make your way up Carrer de Sant Miquel towards Carrer de la Missió to pick up lunch from **Simply Fosh** (▷ 40), the city venture by acclaimed chef Marc Fosh in the stunning 17th-century surroundings of the Hotel Convent de la Missió.

Afternoon In the old town, stop at **Can Marquès Contemporáneo** (▷ 33), an elegant townhouse staging temporary art exhibitions, then on to nearby **Casa Olesa** (▷ 33). There are also art galleries and Arab Baths in the surrounding streets. These medieval lanes lead back to **La Seu** (▷ 30–31), Palma's stunning cathedral. You can visit most days of the week; prepare to be surprised by some of the bold additions to the interior. After leaving La Seu look around the outside of **Palau de l'Almudaina** (▷ 26) and **Palau March** (▷ 28).

Dinner Cross Plaça de la Reina and head into **La Llotja** (▷ 34) for pre-dinner drinks and tapas. Mallorcans won't consider eating out before 9pm so there's time to try some of the bars off Carrer Apuntadors. Then head west on foot, across Avinguda Argentina, into Santa Catalina, a neighbourhood crammed with good restaurants.

Evening After dinner return to La Llotja to see if there's a band playing at the **Jazz Voyeur club** (▷ 38).

DAY 2: SÓLLER

Morning Make an early start and drive to **Sóller** (▷ 66–67). The train from Palma (departures daily from 8am, ▷ 119) is a good alternative but limits what you can do during the day. If driving, the road to Sóller is sign-posted from Palma's ringroad, via Bunyola. Stop at the **Jardines d'Alfabia** (▷ 70–71) just outside Bunyola. Choose between the tunnel and toll or the hair-raising drive up and over the Coll de Sóller to the valley beyond.

Lunch In just one day, it would be a mistake to miss **Deià** (▷ 60–61) so turn left and follow signs for the village. In Deià have lunch at **El Olivo** (▷ 76) and take an hour to look around the village; the house of Robert Graves is the principal attraction although the exclusive hotel hideaway **Belmond La Residencia** (▷ 112) has its own appeal.

Afternoon Return to Sóller. The active option is to follow one of the many walking routes around the town. You can even walk from Deià to Sóller across the Tramuntana mountains in about three hours, although easier walks lead up to the picturesque villages of Fornalutx and Biniaraix and down again in about the same amount of time. Alternatively, visit the lighthouse and walkers' mountain refuge of Sa Muleta on Cap Gros, above Port de Sóller.

Dinner Genteel Port de Sóller has numerous restaurants overlooking the enclosed bay and marina; the sunset views are the main attraction of most. Take a walk around the promenade, with the waves lapping at the shingle beach, and take your pick from the bars and restaurants.

Evening Nightlife isn't a strength of the Tramuntana but the luxury hotels of the town, such as Gran Hotel Sóller, will have stylish bars. The closest cultural entertainment is back in Palma.

ESSENTIAL MALLORCA TOP 25

► ► ►

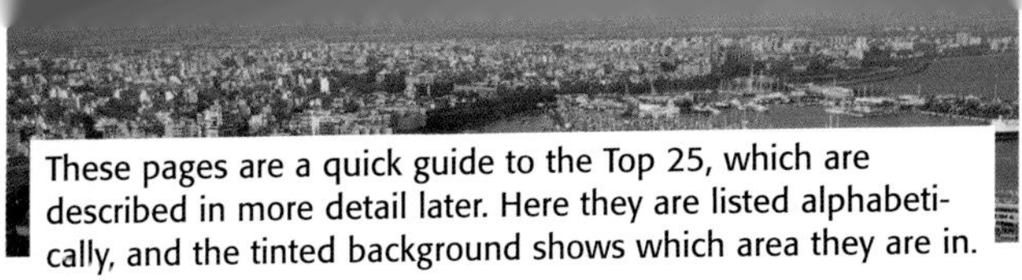

These pages are a quick guide to the Top 25, which are described in more detail later. Here they are listed alphabetically, and the tinted background shows which area they are in.

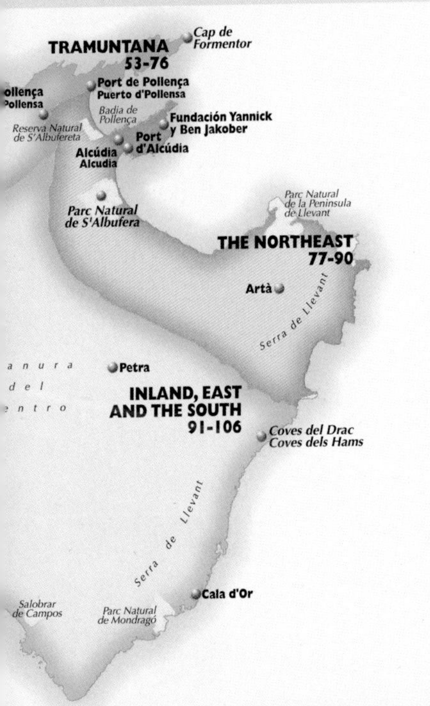

TRAMUNTANA 53–76
Cap de Formentor
Pollença / Pollensa
Port de Pollença / Puerto d'Pollensa
Badia de Pollença
Fundación Yannick y Ben Jakober
Reserva Natural de S'Albufereta
Alcúdia / Alcudia
Port d'Alcúdia
Parc Natural de S'Albufera
Parc Natural de la Peninsula de Llevant

THE NORTHEAST 77–90
Artà
Serra de Llevant

llanura del centro
Petra

INLAND, EAST AND THE SOUTH 91–106
Coves del Drac
Coves dels Hams
Serra de Llevant
Cala d'Or
Salobrar de Campos
Parc Natural de Mondragó

◀◀◀

Shopping

The Balearics have their own distinctly regional products, from shoes to sausages, and shopping for local merchandise is one of the joys of visiting Mallorca. Palma and the towns have lots of independent outlets as well as the major Spanish chainstores and the island's specialties include items crafted from leather, pearls, glass, ceramics and olive wood.

Major Towns
While Palma has the greatest selection of shops on the island—many in the pedestrianized streets of the Old Town—you don't have to go all the way to the capital for good shopping. Mallorcan towns are well used to catering to tourists and locals, although there is considerable variation according to the affluence of the area: upmarket resorts around Palma's bay will have designer brands while working towns such as Manacor and Llucmajor won't.

Leather and Jewellery
But the towns of the interior have other reasons for visiting. Inca, a central industrial town, is known for its leather products. Shoes are made by Camper and Bestard on the island and shops in Inca also sell belts, bags and clothes from retail parks on the outskirts. Manacor has several shops selling the Mallorcan-made pearl jewellery, olive-wood souvenirs and glassware (Majorica and Orquidea are the two leading pearl producers, Lafiore and Gordiola are the two leading

From Manacor pearls to designer bags and shoes, Palma has plenty of great shopping

---

OLIVE OIL

The olive wood utensils hanging in shops around the island are not the only nor the best souvenir produced by the olive groves: that would be Mallorcan olive oil. With such small olive plantations, pure Mallorcan olive oil, under the *Denominació d'origen* label, is relatively expensive but adds interest to salads. The top oil is perhaps Aubocassa from Manacor but Sóller has its own producer, Ca'n Det, where you can see the olives being prepared.

glassware manufacturers—both are popular souvenirs). However, perhaps the most endearing Mallorcan souvenirs are *siurells*. These tiny earthenware figurines have been made in Mallorca since Moorish times. The figures come in a variety of traditional forms, such as a man on a horse or playing an instrument, but all are painted white with red and green flecks of paint. As the name suggests, they are also whistles. The figures are still made in the villages of Sa Cabaneta and Pòrtol.

Food and Drink

While *siurells* are fun, Mallorcan food and drink is much more enjoyable. Mallorca has had something of a gourmet revolution and local products, especially olive oil, wine, pork sausages called *sobrassada,* from the island's indigenous black pigs, almond products and hard cheeses have gained passionate followings. New producers are remaining true to the island's traditions; a gourmet map of the island distributed by the tourist board highlights small-scale producers and you won't find a better memento of Mallorca anywhere. And in every town and village a bakery will dispense *ensaimadas* from first thing in the morning. These pastries, baked in a large, flat spiral, are filled with sweet or savoury fillings and often served with an espresso or a cup of hot chocolate. Another widely available Mallorcan speciality is *herbes*, an aniseed-flavoured and very alcoholic drink sold in bright green bottles; Túnel is a well-known brand.

Look for olive wood, pottery, cheese and dried meats at the local shops and markets

MALLORCAN WINE

The Romans introduced vines to the island but it is only in the last few years that the potential of the Mallorcan wine industry has been realized. A younger generation of winemakers has taken over and they are welcoming visitors to their *bodegas*; the best *bodegas* (wineries) host art shows, tasting events and guided tours. And the wines? Still niche interest for oenophiles but getting better by the bottle.

Staying

Arguably, Mallorca boasts the widest range of accommodation in the Mediterranean, from budget beachside hotels to luxurious hideaways in the hinterland. Whether you want a suite with your own plunge pool or a basic but comfortable cell in a monastery, you can have it on Mallorca.

Book Direct
The internet has helped change the face of tourism on Mallorca. Where once the big beach resorts were the preserve of tour operators, now families are able to find deals for themselves on well-known websites and book a low-cost flight to Palma.

Types of Accommodation
Mallorcan accommodation has diversified in the last decade. The most dramatic growth has been in small rural hotels or converted farm buildings *(fincas)*—these typically offer a handful of stylish rooms, good food, seclusion and plenty of outdoor activities. The town-house hotel has also extended beyond Palma's superb selection to towns like Pollença. But be warned: prices for the new generation of hotels, whether they're the latest beach clubs, or big names such as Belmond La Residencia (▷ 112), are high. A less expensive option, but one valid only for a night at a time, are the mountain refuges along the route of the Ruta de Pedra en Sec walking trail in the Tramuntana mountains (▷ 75).

Accommodation with character: Mallorca can offer it all

PILGRIMS' REST
There's a spiritual streak running right through Mallorca. You can experience this at one of several sanctuaries or monasteries across the island where bedrooms are available overnight for pilgrims and travellers. With most of these sanctuaries, such as the Santuari de Cura (▷ 102), set on top of hills these can be spectacular places to wake up in the morning. Charges are minimal—unless you end up in one of the chic converted convents and hermitages that are now widespread.

Mallorca by Night

Mallorca's nightlife varies according to where you are and the time of year. And, of course, how old you are. Nightclubs in the major resorts cater to younger visitors, but there are plenty of options where beats-per-minute don't matter. Just remember that Mallorcan nights start late and finish in the early morning.

Heading Out
Nightlife in Mallorca goes much deeper than a handful of (pricey) nightclubs. In Palma most nights out begin with a glass of wine or *fino* (dry sherry) at a tapas bar before people settle down in restaurants until 11pm or so. Then the action moves to venues such as the jazz club on Carrer Apuntadors. Outside Palma you can hear live music in venues in surprising locations: Muro is a hotbed of indie bands and techno clubs. Mallorca is also blessed with several excellent festivals which showcase live music (often classical) during the year. And several towns, notably Artà and Alcúdia, have thriving theatres.

What's On
Some hotels, shops and tourist information offices have copies of Mallorcan listings magazines: look out for *Dígame*, which focuses on mainstream theatre and shows, and the *Mallorca Daily Bulletin,* which includes a daily guide to local evenings, including concerts, exhibitions and markets.

CHRISTMAS IN PALMA

Christmas comes to even this sun-kissed Mediterranean city. The shop windows are decorated with sleighs and nativity scenes as the streets fill with shoppers searching out gifts. But at night the city becomes more magical thanks to strings of lights wound around the palm trees on the waterfront and the floodlights giving a golden glow to the most beautiful buildings, including the cathedral. The Christmas lights stay on for December and January, brightening up the darkest months.

Night-time entertainment kicks off late; whether you want dancing, jazz or just a great night out

Eating Out

Today, eating out in Mallorca can be an exciting experience. Admittedly, rustic Mallorcan cuisine has long lacked subtlety but chefs are gradually updating and refining the island's food. The result is Modern *Mallorquin*: local ingredients subjected to a lighter touch. There are also cuisines from all over the world among the hundreds of restaurants on Mallorca so you need never resort to the humble burger and fries.

Great Food

The island has a strong tradition of tasty and hearty cuisine—suckling pig, roast lamb, *arroz brut* ('dirty rice')—but a new generation of chefs has taken the best of the local ingredients to produce dishes that are lighter and influenced by the rest of the Mediterranean. Of course, it is very difficult to improve on some Mallorcan specialties. *Pa amb oli*, crusty slices of bread rubbed with garlic, ripe tomato and served with olive oil, proves that simple dishes can be heavenly. Almond cake makes a perfect dessert. Other specialties, such as *frito* (diced potatoes fried with chopped offal), stem from Mallorca's frugal, rural past. The Mallorcan restaurant scene changes all the time. Some things are constant: rural towns will usually have an excellent *celler* restaurant, and ports should have a couple of good fish restaurants. The finest restaurants are not always found in Palma; many of the top hotels have outstanding restaurants while other must-visit restaurants may be in out-of-the-way locations.

Good food, great wine and fine dining—Mallorca has something to please everyone

BREAKFAST, LUNCH, DINNER

Mallorcans breakfast lightly: a *café solo* (black) and a sweet pastry might be all that's offered. Lunch is more substantial and can take a couple of hours until 3pm; after all it will have to keep you going until a late supper from 9pm onwards. Look out for the economical *menu del dia*. Don't worry if you get hunger pangs: tapas bars are common across Mallorca and can supply a plate of bite-size snacks and a glass of *cerveza* (beer).

Restaurants by Cuisine

The island has restaurants serving food in many different styles and to suit all budgets. On this page they are listed by cuisine. For a more detailed description of each individual restaurant, see Mallorca by Area.

SEAFOOD

La Parada del Mar (▷ 52)
Peix Vermell (▷ 40)
El Pilón (▷ 40)
Rocamar (▷ 52)

MODERN MALLORCAN

Béns d'Avall (▷ 76)
Casal Santa Eulalia (▷ 90)
Es Faro (▷ 76)
Sa Plaça, Alcúdia (▷ 90)
Sa Plaça, Petra (▷ 106)

ITALIAN

Dolc y Dolc (▷ 106)
La Locanda Paraiso da Massimo (▷ 90)
Mantonia (▷ 90)

Below: One of the restaurants overlooking the water at Port de Pollença

ONE OF A KIND

Jardín (▷ 90)

TRADITIONAL MALLORCAN

Es 4 Vents (▷ 106)
Ca n'Antuna (▷ 76)
Ca'n Pedro II (▷ 39)
Es Celler (▷ 106)
La Fonda (▷ 76)
Es Verger (▷ 76)

MODERN MEDITERRANEAN

La Gran Tortuga (▷ 52)
Es Llaut (▷ 106)
Misa Braseria (▷ 40)
El Olivo (▷ 76)
Restaurante S'hort (▷ 52)
Sadrassana (▷ 40)
Simply Fosh (▷ 40)
La Terrassa (▷ 76)
Las Terrazas de Bendinat (▷ 52)
Sa Vinya (▷ 76)

VEGETARIAN

Bon Lloc (▷ 39)
Dharma Café (▷ 90)

TAPAS

Bar España (▷ 39)
La Bodeguilla (▷ 39)
La Bóveda (▷ 39)
Can a Bel (▷ 106)
El Pilón (▷ 40)

CAFÉ FOOD

Balneario Illetas (▷ 52)
Café Parisien (▷ 90)
C'an Joan de s'Aigo (▷ 39)
+Natural (▷ 40)

SPANISH

Casa Julio (▷ 39)
Montimar (▷ 52)
Es Recó de Randa (▷ 106)

Top Tips For...

However you'd like to spend your time in Mallorca, these ideas should help you tailor your perfect visit. Each suggestion has a fuller write-up elsewhere in the book.

MODERN ART

Encounter quirky installations, sculptures and a full rhinoceros skeleton at the Fundación Yannick y Ben Jakober (▷ 82–83).

Get wet at the cutting-edge Centro Cultural d'Andratx (▷ 48), the only gallery with its own swimming pool.

Visit Es Baluard (▷ 32), Palma's most well-known gallery.

Get familiar with the March family at Palau March (▷ 28).

Trawl the private art galleries of Pollença (▷ 74) and Artà (▷ 88) to find emerging artists.

Stay at Convent de la Missío (▷ 112), one of several hotels in Palma with its own art gallery.

See where abstract expressionist Joan Miró expressed himself at Fundació Pilar i Joan Miró (▷ 44).

History, wine, art...

Buy a bottle of wine from Macià Batle (▷ 100); the labels are by artists commissioned by the *bodega*.

THE BEACH

Saddle up at the Son Menut horse riding centre (▷ 105) for a horse ride along the sands.

Try sailing and watersports at Reial Club Náutico Port de Pollença (▷ 75).

Explore Mondragó marine park (▷ 94), where Playa S'Amarado is rated as one of Europe's best beaches.

Relax at Formentor beach (▷ 56) with a drink from the Hotel Formentor.

SELF-INDULGENCE

Eye up the mouthwatering truffles at Frasquet chocolatier (▷ 37) in Palma.

Book a suite at La Residencia in Deià (▷ 112), hideaway of the rich and famous.

Shop at **Shobha Diane** (▷ 74), a jeweller in Pollença specializing in custom-made amber pieces.
Charter a boat from Marina Yachting (▷ 51) in Port d'Andratx.
Eat at Misa Brasseria (▷ 40), Palma's most fashionable eatery and the latest exciting venture of star chef Marc Fosh.

DINING OUT

Blow the budget at Jardín (▷ 90), a superb Michelin starred restaurant in Port d'Alcúdia.
Eat on the terrace of Es Recó de Randa (▷ 106), one of the best restaurants in the interior.
Check out Santa Catalina (▷ 39), a Palma neighbourhood where restaurants proliferate.
Bar-hop the tapas joints of La Llotja (▷ 39).
Test Es Verger's (▷ 76) reputation for serving the most more-ish roast lamb on the island.

LOCAL CULTURE

Learn about Mallorcan rural life at La Granja (▷ 45), a country estate near the Serra de Tramuntana.
Listen to the choir and explore Monastir de Lluc (▷ 62–63), Mallorca's most sacred spot.

...there's much more to Mallorca than sand, sea and sun

Find out why the Archduke Ludwig Salvador is revered on the island at his house Son Marroig (▷ 71).
Attend a concert at Costa Nord's (▷ 70) summer music festival.
Join in at one of Mallorca's boisterous festivals (▷ 114), such as the Battle of Grapes in Binissalem on the last Sunday in September.
Shop at a weekly local market (▷ 88); market days at Inca and Sineu are big events.

ESSENTIAL MALLORCA TOP TIPS FOR...

USING YOUR LEGS

Walk a section or more of the Ruta de Pedra en Sec (the Dry-Stone Route, ▷ 75), a 150km (93-mile) walking route in the Tramuntana.

Bring a bike or hire one and take to Mallorca's marvellous roads with other cyclists (▷ 51, 104).

Go swimming at a beach (▷ 94)—there are plenty to choose from around three-quarters of Mallorca's coastline.

Climb the 365 steps up to the Calvary chapel (▷ 64–65) in Pollença.

FAMILY FUN

Marvel at the sizes, shapes and hues of the inhabitants of Palma Aquarium (▷ 29).

Scream at the thrills and spills of Aqualand (▷ 51) in S'Arenal, on the bay of Palma.

Go underground at the Coves del Drac (▷ 96–97) and come up smiling.

Go on—do it

HITTING THE HISTORY TRAIL

See Mallorca's history in a single building's architecture at the Palau de l'Almudaina (▷ 26).

Find out who invaded who at the Museu de Mallorca (▷ 25) in Palma.

Go deep into Mallorca's past at the Museu Etnològic de Mallorca (▷ 87).

Walk around Roman ruins at Alcúdia town (▷ 80).

TASTING LOCAL PRODUCE

Sample some of Mallorca's distinctive wines after tours of Jaume Mesquida, Macià Batle and Miquel Oliver (▷ 100).

Buy your fruit and vegetables from the village of Vilafranca de Bonany (▷ 103).

Try local cheese at Formatges Burguera (▷ 105).

Appreciate Mallorca's own black pigs, from which traditional *sobrassada* (spicy pork sausages) are produced.

Mallorca by Area

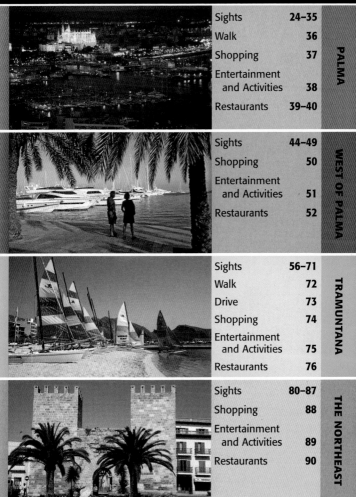

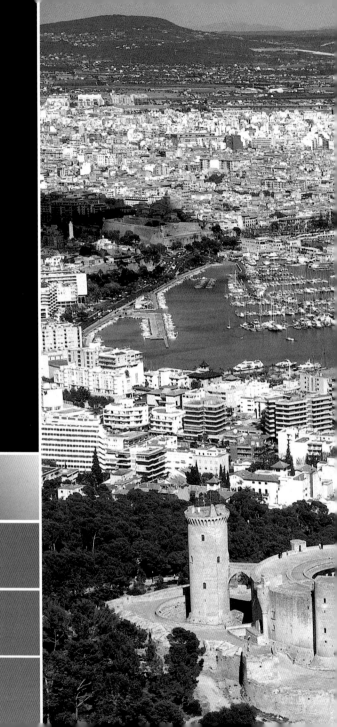

Mallorca's underrated capital surprises with its compact size and delights with a rich array of historic buildings, such as the world-class cathedral, galleries, palaces and family-friendly activities.

5

Ma-1110

Ma-11

PALMA

Poble
Espanyol

Passeig   CaixaForum   Museu d'Art Espanyol
des Born   (Gran Hotel)   Contemporani

Es Baluard   La   Palau   Plaça Major
Passeig   Llotja   March   Basílica de
Marítim   Sant Francesc
              Palau de   Casa Olesa
              l'Almudaina   La   Museu de Mallorca
Castell   Seu   Banys Àrabs
de Bellver
              Museu de Muñecas
El Terreno   de Palma
                              Can Marquès
Son   Contemporáneo
Buit

Ma-20

Ma-13A

Ma-19

Ma-1

Badia de Palma

6

0 ————————— 2 km
0 ————————— 1 mile

Barcelona   Ibiza   Cabr
València   Mene

D

Ma-20

Ma-15

Ma-19

Es Molinar

Coll
d'en Rabassa ■

✈
Aeroport de
Son Sant Joan

● **Palma
Aquarium**

Can Pastilla ■

*Illot de
sa Galera* ▪

*Platja
de Palma*

Castell de Bellver

TOP 25

From left: View over the Bay of Palma from the castle; the colonnades and tower

THE BASICS

www.cultura.palma.es
D6
Carrer Camilo José Cela, 17, Parc Bellver
971 735 065
Castle and museum: Apr–Sep Tue–Sat 8.30–8, Sun 10–8, Mon 8.30–1; Oct–Mar Tue–Sat 8.30–6, Sun 10–6, Mon 8.30–1
3, 21 then 15-min uphill walk, or city sightseeing bus
Inexpensive; free Sun; multilingual audiotours

HIGHLIGHTS

- Classical concerts in the courtyard in the summer.
- Panoramic views of Palma from the roof.

TIP

- If you have a taste for military history, continue to the Museu Militar de Sant Carles, in Carretera Dique del Oeste. The museum has a collection of weaponry in a 17th-century fort.

On the west side of Palma, this carefully preserved 14th-century fort, surrounded by a pine forest, offers an insight into the city's history, an exhibition of classical sculpture and superb views over the bay.

Royal castle Palma's squat, circular castle was built to defend the island's royal family. It was commissioned by King Jaume II in 1300, designed by architect Pere Salva and completed in a mere ten years. However, as a royal residence its days were numbered. For much of its lifetime the castle has been a prison and one of its earliest guests was Jaume IV, imprisoned after the Battle of Llucmajor in 1349.

Prison with a view Castle Bellver has been home to a variety of prisoners, including political prisoners in the Spanish War of Succession, captured French officers, and Republican prisoners during the Spanish Civil War. But in the last couple of decades, the castle has been home to Palma's municipal history museum, which covers the city's Roman, Moorish and modern history. Exhibits are distributed across the City Museum and the Despuig Collection, items gathered by Cardinal Antoni Despuig (1745–1813). However, the principal attraction is Castle Bellver itself. A walk around the courtyard reveals that the circular castle consists of two levels: soldiers lived on the ground floor, the royal family on upper levels. The castle and museum are open daily and there's no charge for visiting on Sundays.

Museu de Mallorca

For a wide-ranging account of Mallorca's varied history visit this 17th-century mansion, which houses the island's most important collections of artefacts spanning 2,500 years.

Marvellous museum Just east of the cathedral, the Museu de Mallorca represents not just the island's Christian history but all periods before and after the Catalan invasion of 1229. The museum building itself is a 17th-century palace, with a whitewashed exterior and low arches. Inside, the galleries are arranged chronologically, starting from the pre-Talaiotic period in the basement and working through the Moorish and Roman occupancies to the upper floors filled with Gothic, Renaissance and baroque religious art.

Prehistoric exhibits No other museum illustrates quite so clearly Mallorca's history as an island of colonists: from the Moors and Romans to the German and British holiday-makers of today. Some of the most interesting exhibits stem from the sophisticated prehistoric Talaiotic culture. Look in particular for the beautifully crafted bronze figurines of warriors, the stand-out exhibits here. Palma was founded in 123BC but the Moors invaded the island in AD902 and remained in control for three centuries; Islamic exhibits include gold coins and jewellery, found in a cave on the island. Join the 20th century and you'll find evidence of Palma's place in Modernism.

THE BASICS

www.museudemallorca.caib.es

➕ e4

✉ Carrer de la Portella, 5

☎ 971 177 838

🕓 Tue–Sat 10–7, Sun 10–2

🚌 2

✋ Inexpensive

HIGHLIGHT

● The Talaiotic and Moorish galleries; focus on these if you're short of time.

TIPS

● Combine the Museu de Mallorca with a visit to one of the merchant's houses nearby, such as Can Marquès (▷ 33), for a fix of Modernism.

● For an extra insight into Mallorca's religious history, visit the nearby Museu Diocesà (Carrer Mirador 1). The museum's highlight is the table of St. George by Pere Niçard.

Palau de l'Almudaina

TOP 25

From left: Statue of Hondero; Mojer's trip-tych; Gothic arches; the palace's exterior

Mallorca's Moorish and Catalan backgrounds come together in this beautiful, enthralling building. Still used as a royal palace, the Palau de l'Almudaina is a highlight of Palma.

Moorish delight Construction of the superb Almudaina began after the Moorish conquest of the island in AD902; the alcazar's foundations and the line of Moorish arches visible from the seafront remain, but the palace has since been rebuilt with Gothic flourishes by the Catalan kings who conquered Mallorca in the 13th century. Jaume II commissioned most of the best work in the 14th century, employing Moorish designers and craftsmen, which explains the Moorish elements of the interior.

Palatial home One of the capital's most important buildings, the Almudaina is nominally still a royal palace, although the Royal family are infrequent visitors. The building is divided into the King's Palace and the Queen's Palace and access is limited to the king's half and some of the shared areas, with most areas of interest reached via the central courtyard, the Patio de Armas. The King's Study is accessed via the Royal Staircase, and is where guests are received at state functions; the throne room is next door. But the best artwork—paintings and religious icons—can be seen in the Capella de Santa Ana, just off the main courtyard. Pre-dating the chapel, the Almudaina's Arab baths were discovered during restoration.

Palau March

From left: Corberó's Orgue del Mar; the palau's main staircase

THE BASICS

www.fundacionbmarch.es

✚ c3

✉ Carrer Palau Reial, 18

☎ 971 711 122

🕐 Apr–Oct Mon–Fri 10–6.30; Nov–Mar Mon–Fri 10–2

🍴 Café (€), access is via Carrer del Conquistador

🚌 2, 15, 25

♿ Moderate

HIGHLIGHT

● Seeing modern art and a new perspective of La Seu with the backdrop of a traditional sandstone building and its Moorish arches.

TIP

● Get a coffee at the Cappuccino Café in the Palau's building and people-watch the main thoroughfare below from the terrace.

The millionaire March family's palatial home is now a modern museum of sculpture with works by big names such as Moore and Rodin. But close-up views of the cathedral steal the show.

A millionaire's mansion Influential, wealthy and very well-connected, the March family had the pick of the real estate when building the family home in the 1940s. They chose a prime location between the Palau de l'Almudaina and La Seu. March senior, Joan (1880–1962), one of the world's richest men, spent a large chunk of his fortune on art. In 2003 the March family's mansion opened to the public, revealing his eclectic art collection. Pieces range from the classic—a bronze by Auguste Rodin, carvings of the Virgin—to the contemporary, including the golden globules of the *Orgue del Mar* by Spanish scupltor Xavier Corberó on the terrace.

Compulsive collectors It's not just sculpture that caught the eye of Joan March and his son, fellow art collector Bartolomé (1917–1988). There's a map room filled with 16th-century charts, many by Mallorcan cartographers. And the collection of Nativity scenes, comprising 2,000 tiny figures, will please some people. Palau March may not be the most amazing private art collection on the island (that's arguably the Yannick and Ben Jakober Foundation, ▷ 82) but it's good value and the superb views of the city make it a worthwhile stop.

From left: The Jungle walkway; one of the tropical displays

Moray eels, sharks and deadly puffer fish: all are safely contained in the spectacular tanks of Palma's superb aquarium. With fascinating indoor and outdoor habitats, the aquarium is an outstanding day out.

Aquatic amazement If you've ever wondered how many hearts an octopus has (answer: three) or why deep-sea creatures are often red (you'll have to visit for the answer), Palma's aquarium is the place to find out. The emphasis here is on wowing visitors with the world's most spectacular and exotic marine life. As you walk through the darkened rooms, your eye is drawn to vivid pinks and neon yellows of tropical fish. Many exhibits have been selected for their quirkiness and beauty: look out for pyjama cardinal fish, troupes of clownfish, angel fish trailing the tips of their tails and tiny, gemlike fish the size of a coin.

Family friendly The tanks—many at a child-friendly height—are organized by the theme of exploration and habitat; there are tropical fish of every hue in the New World section and monstrous lobsters and moray eels lurking in wrecks in the Old World area. But don't think too much about the science—indeed, few of the 700 species are named. If you do want more information, you'll have to ask. The shallow encounter pools have gurnards (flying fish) and slow-moving rays. Outside, rare green and hawksbill turtles live in Turtle Lagoon, while waterfalls cool the misty Jungle walkway.

THE BASICS

www.palmaaquarium.com

🔶 Off map at e5/E6

✉ Carrer Manuela de los Herreros I Sora, 21

☎ 971 702 902

🕐 Jun 15–Sep 15 daily 10–8 (last entrance 6.30pm); Sep 16–Jun 14 10–6 (last entrance 5pm)

🍴 Canteen-style restaurant (€–€€)

🚌 15, 23, get off at Ses Fontanelles

♿ Very good, ramp access throughout

👋 Expensive

❓ There are daily feeding times for the turtles, rays and sharks; check in advance

HIGHLIGHT

● The moray eels are compulsively eerie but for many people the slowly circling sharks in Europe's deepest tank, Big Blue, are the aquarium's highlight. Pull up a cushion and watch them glide by.

La Seu

HIGHLIGHTS

● Look at the contrast between the two chapels beside the High Altar: Miquel Barceló's Capella de Sant Pere and the Capella de la Trinitat, one of the oldest parts of the cathedral.
● Don't miss the elaborate tombs for the royal family.

TIP

● Mass is held at 10.30am and 7pm on Sunday and adds much to the experience.

La Seu is to cathedrals what Picasso is to painting: bold, eye-catching and thoroughly Spanish. Palma's cathedral has a spectacular seafront location and standout features, including a chapel renovated by artist Miquel Barceló.

Stunning spires You can't miss it; even from an aeroplane Palma's cathedral stands out. Up close, it is even more impressive. Firstly, there's the setting, a stone's throw from the sea but still in the heart of the old town, next to the Palau de l'Almudaina. Then there's the architecture. The cathedral was constructed between 1385 and 1430 from the local limestone that has a golden glow at sunset. Tall buttresses reach above palm trees while the two towers on either side of the Portal Mayor frame a

Clockwise from left: The golden pinnacles of La Seu; the steps up to the cathedral; the nave dates from the 14th century; carved stonework above the main entrance; detail from the façade; the cool cloisters are a welcome relief from the summer sun

magnificent rose window 12m (39ft) in diameter, one of the largest in the world. When this main door isn't in use during a service, enter through the Portal de la Almoina on the north side. First impressions are of the vast scale of the nave.

An intriguing interior Between 1904 and 1914 Catalan architect Antoni Gaudí made several modifications to the interior, in particular a canopy over the altar representing the crown of thorns placed on Jesus' head. But another Spanish artist, Mallorca-born Miquel Barceló, has had an even greater impact. From 2001 to 2007 he redecorated the Capella de Sant Pere, on the south side of the nave. His creation—organic, thought-provoking and long overdue—is one of the interior's main attractions.

THE BASICS

www.catedraldemallorca.
info/principal
✚ d4
✉ Plaça Almoina
☎ 902 022 445
🕐 Jun–Sep Mon–Fri
10–6.15, Sat 10–2.15;
Apr–May, Oct Mon–Fri
10–5.15, Sat 10–2.15;
Nov–Mar Mon–Fri 10–3.15,
Sat 10–2.15
🚌 2
♿ Inexpensive

More to See

ES BALUARD

www.esbaluard.org

Mallorca isn't short of contemporary art museums and Es Baluard is arguably Palma's best (although it is eclipsed by Andratx's Cultural Centre, ▷ 48). The first impression is of its magnificent space on the city's walls and the great views of the bay. It's a stimulating setting for the collection of painting, sculpture and installations by leading international artists such as Miró and Barceló.

➕ a3 (fold-out map) ✉ Plaça Porta Santa Catalina, 10 ☎ 971 908 200 🕓 Tue–Sat 10–8, Sun 10–3 💶 Moderate

BANYS ÀRABS

Just within the wall bordering the Old Town, Palma's Arab Baths are one of the few remnants of the island's Moorish period. The baths are thought to date from the 10th century and while they require a little imagination to enjoy these days, the hot room *(caldarium)* clearly illustrates how an underground furnace heated the room

with hot air while a stream, diverted down a channel, created steam.

➕ e5 ✉ Carrer Can Serra, 7 ☎ 637 046 534 🕓 Apr–Nov daily 9–7.30; Dec–Mar 9–6 💶 Inexpensive

BASÍLICA DE SANT FRANCESC

www.franciscanostor.org

As the burial place of the Mallorcan mystic Ramón Llull and with a statue of Mallorcan missionary Junípero Serra (▷ 99) outside, this church is closely connected to the island's history. The basilica is based around the most well-preserved cloisters in Palma, surrounding a large courtyard. The cloisters are Gothic in style but the church's Gothic façade was replaced by a baroque design in the 17th century after being struck by lightning.

➕ f3 (fold-out map) ✉ Plaça de Sant Francesc ☎ 971 262 613 🕓 Mon–Sat 9.30–1, 3.30–6, Sun 9–1 💶 Inexpensive

CAIXAFORUM

www.fundacio.lacaixa.es

One of Palma's finest examples of

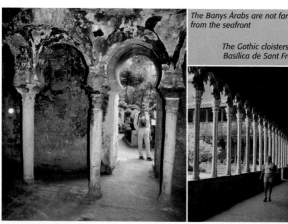

The Banys Àrabs are not far from the seafront

The Gothic cloisters of the Basílica de Sant Francesc

Modernist architecture, the historic Gran Hotel is now used by La Caixa Foundation as an arts centre, with regular exhibitions staged on the upper floors. Mallorcan artists are represented in the permanent collection. The building, designed by the Catalan architect Lluís Domenech i Montaner (1850–1923), dates from 1903—look out for the Modernist flourishes inside and out before having a coffee in the excellent ground-floor café.

🔲 d2 ✉ Plaça Weyler, 3 ☎ 971 178 500 🕐 Mon–Sat 10–9, Sun 10–2 🍴 Café on ground floor (€) 🎟 Free

CAN MARQUÈS CONTEMPORÁNEO

www.canmarquescontemporaneo.net

As a strategic Mediterranean port, Palma was a wealthy city and its merchants enjoyed a high standard of living. Many spent their money on building grand town houses. One example is Can Marquès, in the narrow cobbled lanes behind La Seu. The foundations of the mansion were laid in the 14th century but it wasn't until Don Martin Marquès had made his fortune from Puerto Rican coffee that the building became the elegant example of aristocratic living it is today. The highlight is the internal courtyard with its Modernista staircase but the tour also takes in two public rooms, the private family rooms and the chapel, kitchen and servants' quarters. There are also regular exhibitions of world-class contemporary art.

🔲 d4 ✉ Carrer Zanglada, 2A ☎ 971 716 247 🕐 Mon–Fri 10–3 🎟 Moderate

CASA OLESA

Look through the iron gates of this merchant's mansion in the street next to Can Marquès for a glimpse of Palma's finest patio. The house isn't open to the public but you can see why the aristocratic Catalan Olesa family were proud enough of their elegant patio to hang their coat of arms from the balustrade.

🔲 e4 ✉ Carrer d'en Morey, 9

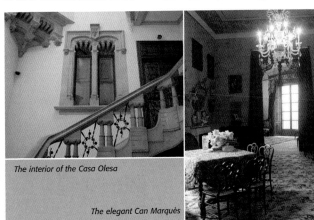

The interior of the Casa Olesa

The elegant Can Marquès

LA LLOTJA

Once the city's stock exchange and guildhall, La Llotja is now a cultural centre with small-scale exhibitions. The main attraction is the building itself, an elegant example of Gothic architecture dating from the 15th century, resembling a castle with its turrets and a church with its gargoyles. La Llotja looks out on a small square close to the port and is surrounded by bars and restaurants.

⊞ b4 (fold-out map) ✉ Plaça de la Llotja ☎ 971 711 705 🕐 Tue–Sat 11–2, 5–9, Sun 11–2 ✋ Free

MUSEU D'ART ESPANYOL CONTEMPORANI

www.march.es/arte/palma/

This museum, in an 18th-century mansion close to the Plaça Major, hosts thought-provoking exhibitions alongside its permanent collection of works by key names in Spanish modern art: Picasso, Miró, Dalí and now local artist Miquel Barceló. The wealthy Mallorcan banker and avid collector of artworks, Joan March (▷ 28) commissioned the building and most of the art comes from Fundación Joan March.

⊞ e2 ✉ Carrer de Sant Miquel, 11 ☎ 971 713 515 🕐 Mon–Fri 10–6.30, Sat 10.30–2 ✋ Free

MUSEU DE MUÑECAS DE PALMA

www.palmamuseopepas.com

The antique dolls at the Doll Museum include a large collection from the early to mid-19th century, with Spanish, Italian, Japanese, French and German examples, as well as pre-Columbian dolls made from fabric and wax dolls used as votive offerings in ancient Greece. There are also a couple of Steiff teddy bears here, worth a cool €1,500 each.

⊞ d3 ✉ Carrer Palau Reial ☎ 971 729 850 🕐 Wed–Mon 10–6 ✋ Inexpensive

PASSEIG DES BORN

A broad, partially pedestrianized avenue, Passeig des Born leads from the cathedral and the Palau de

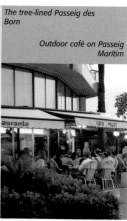

The tree-lined Passeig des Born

Outdoor café on Passeig Marítim

l'Almudaina to the core of the city. It's not a long walk; on the west side you can follow Carrer Apuntador into a neighbourhood thick with tapas bars. At the top, turn left for the grand shops on Jaume III or the narrow lanes of Palma's Old Town.

➕ c3 🍴 Restaurants and cafés

PASSEIG MARÍTIM

Much work has been done on the Passeig Marítim, Palma's seafront promenade, which curls around the bay. The cycle lanes now extend to Can Pastilla to the east and if you have the time you can walk towards Castle de Bellver (▷ 24) on the west side of the bay. The busiest stretch is adjacent to the port, where the marina and nightclubs are located. Between the cathedral and the Passeig Marítim, the Parc de la Mar is an angular, 1960s-era lake. There is plenty of seating so you can admire the mural by Lluís Castaldo on the park wall.

➕ a3 (fold-out map) 🍴 Restaurants, cafés and bars

PLAÇA MAJOR

As it is one of the social hubs of the city, most visitors pass through the Plaça Major in the heart of the Old Town at some point. On the way past the busy outdoor cafés they'll also pass mime artists, buskers and market stalls at the weekends (daily in summer). The square dates from the 19th century and was built on the site of the headquarters of the Spanish Inquisition.

➕ e2 🍴 Restaurants and tapas bars

POBLE ESPANYOL

www.poble-espanyol.com

If you've never seen the Alhambra Palace of Granada or Cordoba's beautiful Moorish buildings, you can see them all, and many other famous Spanish buildings at Poble Espanyol. This collection of reproductions includes houses, castles, churches and palaces, as well as demonstrations by craftspeople.

➕ D5 ✉ Carrer Poble Espanyol, 39 ☎ 971 737 075 🕐 Daily 9–7 🚌 50 💰 Moderate

The open expanse of Plaça Major is at the heart of Palma

Poble Espanyol is a great place to explore Spanish architecture

Palma: Ancient and Modern

Dig into the rich vein of Modernist architecture in Mallorca's compact capital, interspersed with some artistic and historic diversions.

DISTANCE: 2.5km (1.5 miles)   **ALLOW:** 1.5 hours

START

JUNCTION OF CARRER APUNTADORS ON PLAÇA REINA
🚏 c3 🚌 15

END

JUNCTION OF CARRER APUNTADORS ON PLAÇA REINA

PALMA WALK

① With your back to the Palau March gallery, follow Carrer Apuntadors through the tapas quarter of Palma, a neighbourhood now boasting two designer hotels (including Hotel Tres ▷ 111) as well as Palma's most extravagant bar, Abaco (▷ 38).

② As the lane narrows, turn left then right down Sant Pere. This street leads out into the gardens surrounding Es Baluard (▷ 32), central Palma's finest contemporary art gallery.

③ Without crossing the pedestrian bridge, follow Carrer Polvora, leaving the gardens to the left, as the road turns in to the Passeig de Mallorca.

④ Keep to the right and then turn right down Avinguda Jaume III. Follow Palma's top shopping street downhill to the Plaça del Mercat, with two Modernist mansions and the famous chocolatier Frasquet (▷ 37).

⑧ Cross Plaça Cort and leave by Carrer Palau Reial, which brings you past an old-fashioned shopping arcade to Palau March and Palau de l'Almudaina again.

⑦ Head out of the square to the far right, down Carrer Jaume II. At the corner of the Plaça Cort, on your left, and the pedestrianized zone, Can Corbella is perhaps Palma's earliest example of Modernism.

⑥ Follow the Forn del Raco right into the small Plaça Marques where Palma's most elaborate Modernist building, Can Forteza Rey, lies.

⑤ Continue past Plaça del Mercat to the Plaça de Weyler where the distinctive façade of the Forn d'es Teatre (▷ 37) *ensaimada* shop lies opposite the CaixaForum (▷ 32), once the Gran Hotel, Palma's first Modernist building.

Shopping

BONDIAN LIVING STORE

www.bondianliving.com
Set in a wonderful historic building, this interior design and homewares store sells toiletries, ceramics and decorative items. There is even a coffee bar, if you need a break from browsing.
🔲 d3 ✉ Carrer Can Veri, 5
☎ 971 425 180 ⏰ Mon–Sat 10–8

CAMPER

www.camper.com
This popular shoe chain began its life in Mallorca.
🔲 d3 ✉ Avinguda Jaume III, 16 ☎ 971 714 635
⏰ Mon–Sat 10–8

LA CASA DEL MAPA

www.casadelmapa.imi.palma demallorca.es
With maps old and new of the island, you need never get lost again.
🔲 d3 ✉ Carrer Santo Domingo, 11 ☎ 971 225 945
⏰ Mon–Fri 9.30–2, 4.30–7.30

COLMADO SANTO DOMINGO

www.colmadosantodomingo.com
Stock up on spicy *sobrassada* and other Mallorcan specialties at this tiny grocery shop.
🔲 d3 ✉ Carrer Santo Domingo, 1 ☎ 971 714 887
⏰ Mon–Sat 10–8

EL CORTE INGLÉS

www.elcorteingles.es
This central Palma branch of Spain's leading department store stocks

everything from designer clothes to electronics.
🔲 c2 ✉ Avinguda Jaume III, 15 ☎ 971 770 1 / /
⏰ Mon–Sat 10–8

FORN D'ES TEATRE

www.forndesteatre.com
This iconic patisserie is as famous for its art deco façade as its excellent *ensaimadas*.
🔲 d2 ✉ Plaça Weyler, 9
☎ 971 715 254 ⏰ Daily 8–8

FRASQUET

www.confiteriafrasquet.com
Be tempted by Mallorca's finest artisan chocolates in this historic chocolatier.
🔲 d2 ✉ Carrer Orfila, 4
☎ 971 721 354 ⏰ Daily 7.30–2, 5–8

ORQUIDEA

www.perlasorquidea.com
Mallorca's pearls are crafted into necklaces,

TOP SHOPPING

Palma's best shopping streets are concentrated in a small area. To the west of the Passeig des Born, designer outlets line the Avinguda de Jaume III; venture up Carrer Bonaire for more. To the east of the Born, Palma's Old Town is packed with boutiques, jewellers and quirky independent shops. North of the Plaça Major lies the most traditional shopping area, revolving around the Mercat de l'Olivar—this is where you'll find household items and food.

earrings and other jewellery. There's another outlet on Avinguda Jaume III.
🔲 e3 ✉ Carrer Cadena, 3
☎ 971 718 013 ⏰ Mon–Fri 9.30–7.30, Sat 9.30–1.30

PICAROL

Abarcas—Menorcan open-toed sandals—make good beachwear, also available for kids.
🔲 e2 ✉ Carrer Forn del Racó, 1 ☎ 971 711 196
⏰ Mon–Fri 10.30–8, Sat 10.30–noon, 2–8

TARA'S

www.tarasart.es
Tara's sells beautiful leather bags made by local designer Tara Salgad in her workshop in Inca.
🔲 b3 (fold-out map)
✉ Carrer Constitución, 7
☎ 607 118 393 ⏰ Mon–Sat 10–6

TREE OF LIFE

www.treeoflife.es
The place to go for boho-chic women's fashions in light-as-a-feather linens. The shop also sells funky accessories.
🔲 b3 (fold-out map)
✉ Carrer Sant Joan, 3
☎ 971 721 475 ⏰ Mon–Sat 10.30–8

ZARA

www.zara.com
Women's and children's fashions from this much-praised Spanish chain. Menswear outlet is on Plaça Juan Carlos I.
🔲 c3 ✉ Passeig des Born, 25 ☎ 971 719 828
⏰ Mon–Sat 10–9

PALMA SHOPPING

Entertainment and Activities

ABACO

www.bar-abaco.es
Embrace your decadent side with a drink at Palma's most elaborate and surreal nightspot. The interior courtyards and rooms of this mansion have been decorated with cascading flowers and fruit while candles and mirrors lend an air of faded glamour.

➕ b3 (fold-out map)
✉ Carrer Sant Joan, 1
☎ 971 714 939

AUDITORIUM DE PALMA

www.auditoriumpalma.es
Mallorca's largest auditorium has an annual programme of concerts and theatre.

➕ Off map at a3 (fold-out map) ✉ Passeig Marítim, 18
☎ 971 734 735

CITY SIGHTSEEING BUS

www.city-sightseeing.com
See Palma's main sights from a double-decker bus. Tours last 80 minutes and the commentary is in eight languages.

➕ c4 ✉ Avinguda Antonio Maura ⏰ Daily all year

HIPÓDROM SON PARDO

www.hipodromsonpardo.com
Trotting races (carreras) with a horse and trap are the most popular form of horse racing in the Balearics—see and bet on races at Palma's hippodrome.

➕ Off map at d1
✉ Carretera Palma–Sóller km3 ☎ 971 763 853
⏰ Winter Sun pm, summer Fri evening

JAZZ VOYEUR CLUB

www.jazzvoyeurfestival.com
In the heart of the tapas quarter, this intimate, first-floor jazz club has a fantastic vibe and attracts leading acts, such as Diana Krall. An annual August jazz festival is one of Palma's cultural highlights.

➕ b3 (fold-out map)
✉ Apuntadores, 5 ☎ 971 720 780

MARINELAND

www.marineland.es
A great day out for all the family just 10 minutes' drive or bus ride out of Palma. Check out the dolphins, sea lions, penguins, exotic birds and much more. The children's water park adds to the fun.

➕ D6 ✉ Calle Garcilaso de la Vega, 9, Costa d'en Blans ☎ 971 675 125
⏰ Daily 9.30–5.30. Dolphin shows 11.30–3.30. Parrot shows 10.30, 1, 4.30
🚌 L100/2/3/4/6/7/11

PACHA MALLORCA

www.pachamallorca.es
While the best-known Pacha club is in Ibiza, this one (opened in 2013) has to rate a close second with theme nights, sophisticated bars, international DJs, fabulous sound system and lighting, and a super-cool clientele.

➕ Off map at a3 (fold-out map) ✉ Passeig Marítim, 42
☎ 687 570 102

PURO BEACH

www.purobeach.com
For a night of laidback grooves join the beautiful people partying at the Puro hotel every night. DJs range from jazz to deep house.

➕ C3 ✉ Monte Negro, 12, Bay of Palma ☎ 971 425 450

REAL CLUB NÁUTICO DE PALMA

www.rcnp.es
Palma's yacht club celebrated its 60th anniversary in 2008 with a series of regattas. Visitors can learn to sail or canoe at the club.

➕ b4 (fold-out map)
✉ Muelle de San Pedro
☎ 971 726 848

NIGHTLIFE

Palma may not have the depth of entertainment that's available in Madrid or Barcelona but it certainly offers a little bit of everything. It's the island hotspot for tapas and then, depending on your taste, you can move on to the theatre, a small but perfectly formed jazz club or the nightclubs along the seafront; just remember that these don't get going until midnight and may be closed during the winter months.

Restaurants

BAR ESPAÑA (€)

Hidden down a side street in Palma's historic centre, this unpretentious tapas bar serves Basque-style *pintxos* (small pieces of bread with tasty toppings) and tapas. Craft beers are also on offer, as well as excellent wines by the glass. Bring your phrasebook to decipher the chalkboard menu.
🔼 e2 (fold-out map) ✉ 971 724 234 🕐 Mon–Sat dinner, open till late

LA BODEGUILLA (€€)

www.la-bodeguilla.com
Dimly lit, with a moody atmosphere, La Bodeguilla is the perfect place to sample some classic tapas. Try *patatas bravas* (fried potatoes with a spicy tomato sauce), Manchego cheese and *tortilla* (potato omelette); or for something more substantial, paella or braised pork cheeks.
🔼 c2 ✉ Carrer Sant Jaume, 1–3 ☎ 971 726 090 🕐 Daily lunch and dinner

BON LLOC (€€)

www.bonllocrestaurant.com
Palma's longstanding vegetarian restaurant is as popular as ever, with chef Jaunjo Ramírez creating tasty, light dishes from the freshest ingredients.
🔼 c3 ✉ Carrer Sant Feliu, 7 ☎ 971 718 617 🕐 Mon–Wed lunch, Thu–Sat lunch and dinner

LA BÓVEDA (€–€€)

La Bóveda is everything a tapas bar should be: the aroma of cured ham hanging in the air, small glasses of red wine or *fino* on the tiled counter and a loyal band of regular customers. There are also full meals such as steaks or grilled fish. There's a sister bar Taberna de la Bóveda at Passeig Sagrera, 3.
🔼 b4 (fold-out map) ✉ Carrer Boteria, 3 ☎ 971 714 863 🕐 Daily lunch and dinner

WHERE TO EAT

Palma is a compact city but the most established foodie quarter is Santa Catalina, a grid of streets on the west side of Avinguda Argentina where more than 20 restaurants offer cuisines from Italian and Spanish to vegetarian or Vietnamese. Key streets include Fábrica and Soler. It's a shorter walk for a great choice of tapas: just follow Carrer Apuntadores and you'll be in the heart of La Llotja, Palma's tapas quarter. Another foodie enclave at the top of the Passeig des Born is centred on Carrer Sant Feliu.

CA'N JOAN DE S'AIGO (€)

There is a steady bustle of regulars at this landmark café. Dating from 1700, it is the place to come for classic Mallorcan *ensaimadas* (spiral-shaped filled pastries). The art deco interior with its marble-topped tables, chandeliers and original tiles is wonderfully atmospheric. The choice of both sweet and savoury pastries is superb (try the pumpkin), and the ice creams and classic cakes are equally mouthwatering.
🔼 e3 (fold-out map) ✉ Carrer Can Sanç, 10 ☎ 971 710 759 🕐 Daily breakfast, lunch and dinner

CA'N PEDRO II (€€)

www.mesoncanpedro.com
Since 1976 Ca'n Pedro has been delighting diners with hearty Mallorcan cooking. All the island's rustic specialties are available: suckling pig, roast shoulder of lamb, snails and *pa amb oli*.
🔼 Off map at a2 (fold-out map) ✉ Carrer Rector Vives, 14, Genova ☎ 971 402 479 🕐 Thu–Tue lunch and dinner

CASA JULIO (€–€€)

If you are looking for traditional local cuisine (and excellent house wine) then follow the locals to Casa Julio, just west of Carrer Argenteria. It has an inexpensive daily menu, with an emphasis on local produce. Snag a

table on the street for the best atmosphere.
🏠 e3 (fold-out map) ✉ Carrer Prevision, 4 ☎ 971 710 670 🕐 Mon–Sat lunch and dinner

MISA BRASERIA (€€–€€€)

www.misabraseria.com
The latest venture of Michelin-starred chef Marc Fosh, this Mediterranean-style brasserie has a contemporary, welcoming feel. The menu changes seasonally but you can expect innovative combinations like fried pizza with sun-dried tomatoes, fresh figs and Serrano ham, and gazpacho of watermelon and strawberries. The desserts are sublime, with added art-on-a-plate appeal. Head for the plant-filled covered terrace but reserve in advance, especially in mid-summer, when people flock here from all over the island.
🏠 e1 (fold-out map) ✉ Carrer de Can Maçanet, 1 ☎ 971 595 301 🕐 Mon–Sat lunch and dinner, Sun dinner

+NATURAL (€–€€)

www.masntrl.com
Healthy food need not be dull, as +Natural sets out to prove with a selection of salads, stir fries and sweet desserts. Its location makes the café a good spot for lunch and people-watching from the outdoor tables.

🏠 Off map at f1 (fold-out map) ✉ Plaça d'Espanya, 8 ☎ 971 722 232 🕐 Mon–Sat lunch and dinner

PEIX VERMELL (€€–€€€)

www.peixvermell.com
Seafood lovers should seek out Peix Vermell: its salt-encrusted *dorado* (sea bream) is legendary. Other dishes include pasta with clams, lobster stew and a traditional paella. The vaulted ceiling and candlelit tables create an intimate atmosphere, and its wine list is reputedly the best in town.
🏠 a3 ✉ Carrer Montenegro, 1 ☎ 971 079 374 🕐 Daily lunch and dinner

EL PILÓN (€–€€)

www.elpilonmallorca.com
Choose your tapas from the counter in front of the stoves and the chefs will cook it while you wait;

STAR CHEFS

Chefs come and go but a few have stayed the course and can now be considered part of the Palma furniture. Marc Fosh's empire is slowly expanding into the city, with his restaurants Misa Braseria and Simply Fosh. Another veteran member of the international brigade is Koldo Royo from the Basque country. Juanjo Ramírez introduced high-class vegetarian cuisine to the capital with Bon Lloc.

---

seafood is a speciality and the day's catches are laid out before you. This tapas bar, at the top of the Born, is decorated with marine paraphernalia.
🏠 c2 ✉ Carrer Cancifre, 4 ☎ 971 717 590 🕐 Mon–Sat lunch and dinner

SADRASSANA (€€)

www.restaurantsadrassana.com
On the bustling Plaça Drassanes, this venue doubles as a gallery, so you can enjoy looking at the works of art over a pre-dinner cocktail. The Mediterranean-style dishes are prepared with innovative flair and include fresh seafood, grilled meats and lighter vegetarian dishes. It's very popular: book in advance or be prepared to wait a while for a table.
🏠 b3 (fold-out map) ✉ Plaça Drassanes, 15 ☎ 971 728 515 🕐 Daily dinner

SIMPLY FOSH (€€)

www.conventdelamissio.com
Star chef Marc Fosh opened this restaurant in 2009 in the refectory of the Hotel Convent de la Missió. Fosh's innovative cuisine takes on a thoroughly casual style here, going back to simple basics, providing healthy food at affordable prices. The standard is impeccable, the food delicious.
🏠 e1 ✉ Carrer de la Missió, 7 ☎ 971 227 347 🕐 Daily lunch and dinner

This is perhaps the most affluent corner of Mallorca, a magnet for celebrities and sailors. The bay of Palma has resorts with mass appeal and chic enclaves such as Puerto Portals. But venture inland and the rural pace of life remains in the foothills of the Tramuntana.

Sa Marina
Port de Valldemossa

Cala Gata

Son Coll

George Sand

Son n'Olésa

Son Ferrandell

561 Claret

Nova Valldemossa

595

Moleta de Son Cabaspre

34 **La Granja**

nícia

Esporles
Esporlas

Ma-1120

Ses Rogetes

ramuntana

Ma-1041

Ma-1040

Ma-1110

Establiments Nous

Son Espanyol

Puigpunyent
Puigpuñent

Establiments

14 uig de a Baucà

Son Serralta

Es Secar de la Real

Son Anglada

Son Roca- Son Ximelis

Son Vida

Sa Vileta

Ma-20

Fundació Pilar i Joan Miró

486 ▲
Puig Gros de Berdinat

Génova

Costa d'en Blanes

Sant Agustí

Cala Major

Ma-1

Ma-1C

Costa de Berdinat

Platja de ses Illetes

Portals Nous

Illa de sa Torre

Palma Nova

Son Maties

Torre Nova
Magaluf

Illa de sa Porrassa

B a d i a   d e   P a l m a

Badia de Palma

Cap des Falcó

Sol de Mallorca

Illot del Sec

Portals Vells

Cap de Cala Figuera

D   E

West of Palma

Fundació Pilar i Joan Miró

From left: The fundació *from above; Miró's artworks are on display inside and out*

THE BASICS

http://miro.palma
demallorca.es/

⊞ D6

✉ Carrer Joan de Saridakis, 29, Cala Major, Palma

☎ 971 701 420

◉ Mid-May to mid-Sep Tue–Sat 10–7, Sun 10–3; mid-Sep to mid-May Tue–Sat 10–6, Sun 10–3

♿ Moderate

🍴 Café in garden (€)

🚍 3, 6 from Palma

HIGHLIGHT

● Inspired by Miró's graphics? Join a printmaking workshop to learn how to produce your own works of art, part of the *fundació*'s annual summer programme of events for families. The cost of materials is included in the course fee. See the website for more information.

See the studio where artist Joan Miró created some of the 20th century's most distinctive paintings. The *fundació* displays 130 of Miró's artworks and explains how Mallorca inspired many of them.

Mallorca's adopted artist Born in Barcelona but married to a Mallorcan, Pilar Juncosa, artist Joan Miró (1893–1983) eventually settled in Cala Major in 1956. By then he had established himself as a leading contemporary painter and sculptor, producing distinctive abstract works. His workshop was designed by friend and architect Josep Lluís Sert and is distinctively Modernist. On Miro's death the workshop was donated to the Palma City Council and the Fundació Pilar i Joan Miró was created to encourage young artists and explore Miró's work and life.

A shrine to Modernism The complex is much more than a museum, although there are more than 2,500 of his works stored here. The headquarters of the *fundació* was designed by architect Rafael Moneo and has a programme of temporary exhibitions. The Moneo building is surrounded by a sculpture park and beautifully landscaped gardens; in later years Miró became increasingly absorbed in sculpture and the *fundació* concentrates on the last 20 years of his life. The Sert workshop, almost untouched since Miró's death, lies between the main building and Son Boter, his 17th-century farmhouse, and even here he left his mark with etchings on the walls.

La Granja

From left: La Granja's central courtyard; a costumed artisan; explore the grounds

Once a grand country estate with orchards and gardens, La Granja is now a rewarding museum of traditional rural life on Mallorca. Learn more about local foods and farming before touring the mansion.

The good life Before the arrival of the first tourists, Mallorca was a rural idyll where farmers grew enough to feed themselves and sell a bit at the market, as described in Gordon West's memoir of the island in the 1920s, *Jogging Around Majorca*. The landowners ran large, diverse estates and La Granja is an example of one of the largest on Mallorca. The estate dates back to the Catalan conquest of Mallorca in the 13th century, and the country house has been in private hands since 1447. Today, it offers an interesting, if slightly contrived, insight into traditional rural crafts and lifestyles. Visitors can tour the grand house. It's worth seeing how closely home life and food were interlinked: there's an olive mill and a wine press on the ground floor. A darker side to the estate is revealed in the basement: a torture chamber and prison.

Folk fiesta Outside, in the bright daylight, La Granja's gardens are wonderful for children to explore. You might encounter farm animals, including the famous black pig of Mallorca from which *sobrassada* and *botifarra* is produced, and see wild Mallorcan plants such as pines, rosemary and wild asparagus. There are also displays of the work of blacksmiths, cobblers, weavers and carpenters as well as jams and pastries to taste.

THE BASICS

www.lagranja.net
+ D4
⊠ Carrer Esporles–Banyalbufar
☎ 971 610 032
🕐 Daily 10–7
🍴 Restaurant serving Mallorcan dishes (€€)
💰 Expensive

HIGHLIGHT

● Twice weekly (Wed and Fri at 3.30) there's a folklore show with musicians and dancers in traditional costume. As they perform dances and songs from Mallorca's rural festivals, try some of the Mallorcan food prepared for the occasion.

TIP

● As tempting as the local products sold here might appear, you'll find more competitive prices in Tramuntana towns such as Sóller.

Palma Nova and the Bay of Palma

● For beaches, try Ses Illetes and Portals Vells to the west.
● For nightlife, Portitxol offers hipper venues than Magaluf or s'Arenal—but you'll pay more for mixing in fashionable circles.

TIP

● During the summer, parking can be very difficult in the resorts. Try to take one of the many bus services that run around the edge of the bay.

From brash and boisterous Magaluf to the rarefied surroundings of Puerto Portals and Portals Nous, Palma's sweeping crescent bay is large enough for everyone. The high-rise hotels are being replaced by low-rise accommodation.

The tourist invasion You can chart the development of modern Mallorca from a Balearic haven for artists and royalty to package-holiday destination par excellence (2.3 million Briton's visited the island in 1970 and 9 million tourists now arrive annually) by travelling along the Bay of Palma (Badia de Palma). Thankfully, the high-rise towerblocks are gradually being replaced by more sympathetic developments. But the bay remains the hub of Mallorca's tourist industry and you'll find everything here from

beaches packed with sunbathers and theme parks to exclusive hideaways where million-dollar yachts bob in marinas.

Changing tastes In general, the east side of the bay, towards s'Arenal, is favoured by German visitors and the west side, towards Magaluf, by the British. Traditionally, the most upmarket resorts have been to the west: Puerto Portals and Portals Nous. But Portitxol is now fashionable with the young and beautiful who party at its beach club hotels until dawn. An older crowd, including millionaires and celebrities, favours Puerto Portals. Ses Illetes and Palma Nova are two of the most family-oriented areas of the bay's west side. Magaluf is one of Spain's busiest resorts; while Portals Vells is how the bay used to look before package tourism.

THE BASICS

➕ C6–D6

ℹ️ Magaluf: Carrer Pere Vaquer Ramis, 1, tel 971 131 126

ℹ️ Illetes: Passeig d'Illetes, 4, tel 971 402 739

ℹ️ Santa Ponça: Via Puig de Galatzó, 1, tel 971 691 172

🍴 Numerous, many expensive

🚌 From Palma: 15 to s'Arenal. L102 to Port d'Andratx. L104 to Peguera, L105 and L106 to Magaluf

More to See

ANDRATX

The largest inland town in the region is Andratx. It's principal attraction is the outstanding Centro Cultural de Andratx, on the north-west edge of town, which hosts the most exciting contemporary art exhibitions on the island. It is an exceptional venue and worth the drive for anyone with an interest in contemporary art.

➕ B6

Centro Cultural d'Andratx

www.ccandratx.com

✉ Carrer Estanyera, 2 ☎ 971 137 770
🕐 Mar–Oct, Tue–Sun 10.30–7; Nov–Feb Tue–Sun 10.30–4 🍴 Café 💷 Moderate
♿ Good

BANYALBUFAR

Cultivation of the fertile soil around Banyalbufar posed a problem for the early Moorish settlers of Mallorca as the land lay on the steep slopes of the Tramuntana. Their solution was to cut terraces into the mountainsides. The system remains today and is used for gardens, vineyards and vegetable crops. The signs are that Banyalbufar will become as popular as Deià, a short drive north. For now though, it remains a quiet, appealing village with unbeatable views out to sea.

➕ C4 🍴 Restaurants, cafés and bars

CALVIÀ

www.visitcalvia.com

The capital of the Calvià region is an unassuming but affluent place. Key sights include the Romanesque church of San Joan Baptista and Es Capdella, a small village surrounded by almond and carob plantations.

➕ C6 ℹ Passeig del Mar, 13, Calvia
☎ 971 682 365

PARC NATURAL DE SA DRAGONERA

The uninhabited island, lying 1km (0.6 mile) off the western tip of Mallorca, became a nature reserve in 1995, although it was first occupied by environmentalists protesting against mass tourism in

Castell Son Mas in Andratx

Terraces cut into the hillside near Banyalbufar

1977. You reach the island, a haven for seabirds, via a boat trip from Sant Elm, a low-key resort with one of the few sandy beaches on this side of the island. Boats depart from the jetty half-hourly from February to October, weather permitting, and land at Cala Lladó where you can pick up route guides for paths around the island.
➕ A5

Cruceros Margarita

www.crucerosmargarita.com
☎ 639 617 545 🕐 Boat departures from Sant Elm 10.15 to 12.30 daily 💰 Moderate

PEGUERA

www.visitcalvia.com
With the advent of the motorway between Palma and Andratx, Peguera fell off the sightseers' itinerary. It remains a large beach resort, popular with German tour operators. One of its main attractions is the Casal de Peguera, a €5-million theatre-auditorium hosting concerts and theatre productions year-round.
➕ C6 ℹ Avenida Peguera, 76, Los Hexagonos, tel 971 687 083

PORT D'ANDRATX

Life in fashionable Port d'Andratx revolves around the marina in this sheltered inlet. The harbour is almost as well groomed as the people strolling along the waterfront or sipping cappuccinos at the numerous cafés.
➕ B6 🍴 Restaurants, cafés and bars

LA RESERVA

www.lareservamallorca.com
A diverting combination of wildlife reserve, adventure course and educational resource, La Reserva stands in the shadow of the Puig de Galatzó. Wildlife includes birds of prey (with daily displays), three brown bears and some goats and ponies. At Refreshing Mountain, ponds fed by waterfalls, you can cool off in the summer (bring your swimwear). Adventure activities include zip wires, rock climbing, canoeing and mountain biking. If you don't have time to explore the mountains, this is a good alternative.
➕ C5 ✉ Puigpunyent ☎ 971 616 622
🕐 Daily 10–6 💰 Expensive

Sa Dragonera rises from the blue waters of the Mediterranean

La Reserva nestles on the slopes of Puig de Galatzó

Shopping

BEDLINGTON BOOKS

This friendly bookshop in a small square behind the seafront sells new and second-hand books in English and German, as well as cards.

🛨 B6 ✉ Plaça Nova, Port d'Andratx ☎ 971 671 046 🕐 Mon–Sat 10–6

BILLY'S EXCLUSIVE

www.billys-fashiongroup.com
Stunning women's designer clothes, selected by the owner straight off the catwalk, featuring creations by Marc Cain and Thomas Roth. Accessories are also available.

🛨 B6 ✉ Avinguda Gabriel Roca, 7, Port d'Andratx ☎ 971 673 451 🕐 Mon–Sat 10–7, Sun 10–2

BOUTIQUE EUROPA

This large sports store carries an extensive range of sportswear, with top brands such as Adidas, Nike and Ralph Lauren. Also the place to come to pick up a pair of designer shades.

🛨 C6 ✉ Avinguda Peguera 45, Peguera ☎ 971 686 214 🕐 Daily 9.30am–11pm

BOUTIQUE GALINDO

Galindo specializes in good-quality accessories, such as gloves and belts, and larger items such as travel luggage—all crafted from Spanish leather.

🛨 C6 ✉ Carrer Puig d'es Galatzó, 6, Santa Ponça ☎ 971 690 474 🕐 Daily 10–2, 4–8

CERÁMICAS CAPRICHOS

Balearic ceramics and glassware, from all the islands, are sold here, with items for the house and garden.

🛨 C6 ✉ Carrer Bulevar de Peguera, 79, Peguera ☎ 971 687 664 🕐 Mon–Sat 10–2, 4–8

GELATERIA CAPRI

Enjoy delicious home-made ice creams straight from the counter, with views across to the marina.

🛨 B6 ✉ Avinguda Almirante Riera Alemany, Port d'Andratx ☎ 971 686 986 🕐 Daily 9–9

MALVASIA DE BANYALBUFAR

www.malvasiadebanyalbufar.com
This wine cooperative, formed in 1995, has reintroduced the Malvasia grape, first introduced by

WHERE TO SHOP

This corner of the island has a split personality. While the coastal towns and resorts, such as Peguera and Port d'Andratx, are filled with chic boutiques, selling clothes, gifts and accessories, the rural towns and villages often offer a more traditional range of shops. If you're after Mallorcan foods, wines and oils, head uphill to places like Banyalbufar. For fashionable outfits and shoes, stick to the seaside streets.

the Romans, to Mallorca. It is now cultivated on the terraces of Banyalbufar. The resulting wines are made for love not money.

🛨 C4 ✉ Esperit Sant, 13, Banyalbufar ☎ 616 537 146 🕐 By appointment

PERFUMERÍA TIN TIN

www.tintin.es
This perfumery group has multiple outlets in Palma Nova, Peguera, Magaluf and Santa Ponça. All the big brands, from Chanel to Clinique—can be found at duty-free prices.

🛨 C6 🕐 Passeig del Mar, 52, Palma Nova ☎ 902 333 001

VINI E OLII

www.vinieolii.com
High-quality and original wine, as well as spirits and gourmet products, are the speciality here. Wines are sourced mainly from Spain, France and Italy by owner Maria Grazia. Regular wine tasting events take place (see website for details).

🛨 B6 ✉ Carrer Fabrica, 16, Port d'Andratx ☎ 971 671 728 🕐 Mon–Sat 11–8

X-TRA MODA

A well-stocked boutique exuding a urban-chic feel, X-tra Moda represents mainly national design-ers with an emphasis on women's casualwear in bold colourful designs.

🛨 B6 ✉ Carrer de Isaac Peral, 52, Port d'Andratx ☎ 971 672 207 🕐 Daily 10.30–8

Entertainment and Activities

AQUA MALLORCA DIVERS

www.aqua-mallorca-diving.com
This well-established scuba-diving outfit has boat trips out to Sa Dragonera. Shuttles to and from hotels in the area can be arranged.
B6 ✉ Carrer Almirante Riera Alemany, 23, Port d'Andratx ☎ 971 674 376

BARRACUDA

One of the most established and best-known nightclubs in Port d'Andratx, Barracuda hosts a regular line-up of top international DJs, as well as live music and theme nights.
B6 ✉ Carretera de es Port 118 23, Port d'Andratx ☎ 971 673 606

BCM

www.bcmplanetdance.com
One of Europe's largest nightclubs, BCM is in Magaluf. It packs in 5,500 people, dancing to house and techno—which will tell you if it's the place for you.
C6 ✉ Avinguda S'Olivera, Magaluf ☎ 971 132 715

DIABLITO

www.diablitofoodandmusic.com
There are branches of this trendy bar-restaurant-club in Puerto Portals, Santa Ponça, Porto Pí and Port d'Andratx. The lounge club vibe is created by low lighting, plenty of comfortable seating and some fabulous cocktails.

The Porto Pí bar has a terrace.
C6 ✉ Porto Pí, Local 405 ☎ 971 701 414

GOLF FANTASIA

www.golf-fantasia.com
Mallorca's biggest mini-golf course, with three landscaped, 18-hole courses set in tropical gardens, is just behind the seafront road in Palma Nova.
C6 ✉ Carrer Tenis, 3, Palma Nova ☎ 971 135 040 🍴 Café-bar 🚌 L105, L106, L107 from Palma 💶 Moderate

GOLF SANTA PONÇA

www.habitatgolf.es
There are three courses, two of 18 holes and a 9-hole course, of which Santa Ponça I is one of the oldest and most

celebrated on Mallorca. Book in advance.
C6 ✉ Avinguda del Golf, Santa Ponça ☎ 971 699 064 🍴 Restaurant with terrace 💶 Green fee €270

GRAN FOLIES BEACH CLUB

www.granfolies.net
Enjoy a sundowner at this secluded beach club among the rocky inlets south of Port d'Andratx.
B6 ✉ Cala Llamp Port d'Andratx ☎ 971 671 094

MARINA YACHTING

www.marinayachting.net
Learn the ropes at this Royal Yachting Association-approved sailing school in Port d'Andratx's marina. Speedboats and yachts are also available for charter by the day or longer.
B6 ✉ Avinguda Mateo Bosch, Centro Comercial 'Ses Velas', Local 15, Port d'Andratx ☎ 971 672 829

RAD-INTERNATIONAL

www.rad-international.de
Cycling is an increasingly popular activity on Mallorca and you can rent good road or mountain bikes in the southwest of the island from this company. Package deals are also available.
Various locations:
✉ Hotel RIU, Camp de Mar: 971 235 200
✉ Hotel Punta del Mar, Santa Ponça: 971 692 953
✉ Clubhotel Valentin Park, Peguera: 971 032 022 💶 From €15 per day

Restaurants

PRICES

Prices are approximate, based on a 3-course meal for one person.

€€€	over €40
€€	€20–€40
€	under €20

BALNEARIO ILLETAS (€€)

www.balnearioilletas.com
Overlooking a tiny bay, this stylish beachclub has a restaurant serving simple starters such as melon with ham and mains such as grilled fish. But an ice cream and cold drink might be more appropriate.

🔢 D6 ✉ Avenida Illetas, 52a, Illetes ☎ 971 401 031 ⏰ Mar–Dec daily lunch and dinner

LA GRAN TORTUGA (€€)

www.lagrantortuga.net
This long-established restaurant at Peguera has wonderful sea views from its south-coast outpost, complemented by a Mediterranean à la carte menu or traditional tapas for smaller appetites.

🔢 C6 ✉ Aldea Cala Fornells, Peguera ☎ 971 686 023 ⏰ Tue–Sun lunch and dinner

MONTIMAR (€€)

Stop at this highly regarded roadside restaurant for classic Spanish cuisine: lamb with rosemary, stuffed red pepper, grilled squid and sardines, sobrassada (local pork sausage) with honey. There's a terrace for catching some sun. Try the restaurant's own Ambari wine, made from Malvasia grapes grown in Montimar's vineyards.

🔢 C5 ✉ Plaça Constitució, 7, Estellencs ☎ 971 618 576 ⏰ Tue–Sun lunch and dinner

LA PARADA DEL MAR (€€)

www.laparadadelmarsanta ponsa.com
The fish and seafood is displayed like a fish-monger's store at this popular, well-established restaurant. Make your choice and just wait for it to be prepared. Food doesn't get much fresher than this.

🔢 C6 ✉ Puid de's Teix, 6, Santa Ponça ☎ 971 592 715 ⏰ Daily lunch and dinner

ETIQUETTE

There are a few restaurants on the island where a dress code is imposed and others where beachwear is prohibited. But in general eating out is a casual affair in Mallorca. The most relaxed places are the rural restaurants and cafés while some of the more upscale hotels have restaurants where you might feel uncomfortable in shorts and a T-shirt. Children are typically very welcome and hotels will inform you if there is a minimum age for young guests.

RESTAURANTE S'HORT (€€–€€€)

www.spcountryclub.com
Healthy eating is the order of the day at the restaurant of the exclusive Santa Ponça Country Club and Spa. The international menu uses the freshest ingredients. There is a pool-side buffet barbecue on Sundays in summer.

🔢 C6 ✉ Santa Ponça Country Club and Spa, Avenida de Golf, 35 ☎ 971 693 634 ⏰ Mon–Sat lunch and dinner. Lunch only Sun

ROCAMAR (€€)

www.rocamar.eu
The waterfront road in the marina is lined with restaurants; Rocamar was one of the first and still specializes in seafood. You can see the fisher-men auctioning the daily catch at the market further up the road.

🔢 B6 ✉ Carrer Almirante Riera Alemany, 27, Port d'Andratx ☎ 971 671 261 ⏰ Mar–Oct daily lunch and dinner

LAS TERRAZAS DE BENDINAT (€€€)

www.hotelbendinat.es
At night the Hotel Bendinat's restaurant has enviable views over its rocky cove from the candlelit terrace. The cuisine is inspired by the Mediterranean and includes Spanish dishes.

🔢 D6 ✉ Carrer Andrés Ferrat Sobral, 1, Portals Nous ☎ 971 675 725 ⏰ Mar–Oct daily lunch and dinner

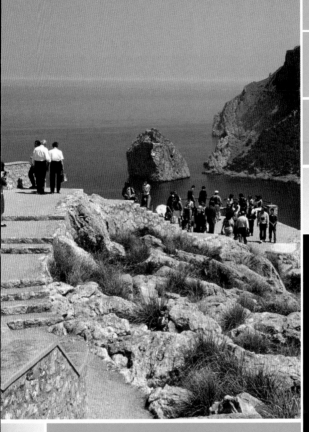

A UNESCO World Heritage Site, the Serra de Tramuntana is an enthralling area of Mallorca, with secluded coves, handsome towns, historic monasteries and fragrant walks through stunning scenery.

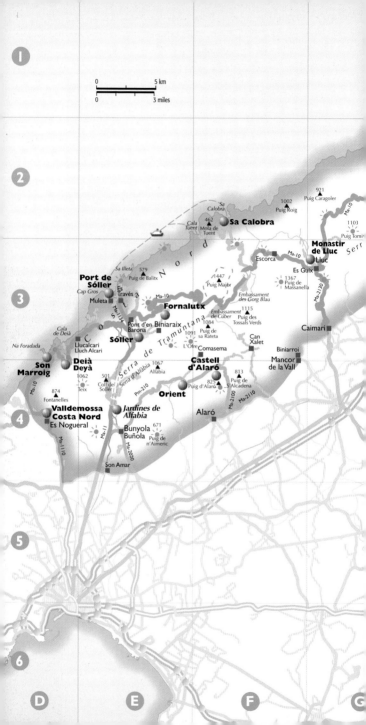

I

0   5 km
0   3 miles

2

Sa Calobra
462 Mola de Tuent
Sa Calobra
Cala Tuent

921 Puig Caragoler

1002 Puig Roig

1103 Puig Tomir

Monastir de Lluc
Lluc

Escorca
Es Guix
Ma-10

Ma-2130

3

Sa Illeta
579 Puig de Balitx

1447
Puig Major

1367 Puig de Massanella

Port de Sóller
Cap Gros
Es Través
Muleta
Ma-11A

Fornalutx
Pont d'en Barona
Biniaraix
Sóller

Embassament des Gorg Blau

Embassament de Cúber
1115 Puig des Tossals Verds

Caimari

Cala de Deià

1091 Puig de sa Rateta
1084
L'Ofre
Comasema

Can Xalet

Biniarroi

Na Foradada

Llucalcari
Lluch Alcari
Deià
1062 Teix
501 Coll del Sóller
Son Marroig

Serra de Tramuntana

1067 Alfàbia
Serra d'Alfàbia

Castell d'Alaró
825 Puig d'Alaró
813 Puig de S'Alcadena

Mancor de la Vall

874 Fontanelles

Valldemossa Costa Nord
Es Nogueral
Ma-1110
Ma-11

Orient

Ma-2100
Ma-2110

Jardines de Alfàbia

Pm-210

671 Puig de n'Aimeric
Bunyola
Buñola
Alaró

Son Amar
Ma-2020

5

6

D   **E**   **F**   **G**

Cap de Formentor

From left: Looking across to Cap de Formentor; tourist signs; dramatic cliffs

THE BASICS

🔲 K1

🍴 Café (€) at the Cap de Formentor and restaurant (€€€) at the Hotel Formentor

🚌 L340 from Palma and Pollença

⛴ Boat from Port de Pollença in summer

Hotel Formentor
www.barceloformentor.com
☎ 971 899 100

HIGHLIGHTS

● Lazing on Formentor beach watching the boats entering and leaving the Bay of Pollença.

● Keep an eye out for the peninsula's birdlife too.

TIP

● To be sure of a parking space at the lighthouse, either leave for Formentor early or arrive late in time for sundown; it's a popular place in the summer.

Hold on to your hats for the daredevil drive along the Cap de Formentor. The rocky peninsula beside Port de Pollença has some spectacular vistas and relatively quiet, sandy beaches backed by fragrant pine forests.

Rugged beauty Spearing out from the northeast corner of the island, the Cap de Formentor has some of Mallorca's most dramatic scenery and best beaches. There's just one road all the way to the tip (the Cap) but the 20km (12.5-mile) drive is entertaining enough for most drivers. From Port de Pollença, follow signs for the Cap de Formentor; the road winds gradually uphill to the Mirador des Colomer, the first of several viewpoints. You can look out over 300m-high (984ft) cliffs teeming with seabirds. At the end of a short path opposite the steps up to the Mirador is a watchtower, the Talaia d'Albercutx. The panoramic views from here take in the whole of the peninsula—then steel yourself for the descent down the other side.

Adrenalin rush The road is very twisty and exposed as it sweeps through dusty pine forests. To the right lies Formentor beach, a narrow, sandy strip which was once owned by the Hotel Formentor. This hotel, now being refurbished after years of decline, was the first luxury resort on the island. It opened in 1929 and has hosted an array of starry guests, from Winston Churchill to Charlie Chaplin. Continue to the end of the road where you'll reach a lighthouse with views to Menorca.

Castell d'Alaró

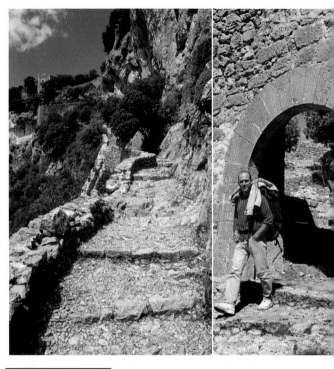

HIGHLIGHT

● Climbing all the way up from Alaró with the prospect of a meal of roasted shoulder of lamb and potatoes at the end in Es Verger. (Take plenty of water and avoid the heat of the day.)

TIP

● If driving up to the car park at Es Verger, be prepared to reverse to allow other cars to pass on corners. This is where renting a small car has its advantages.

One gateway to the Tramuntana range was guarded by this mountaintop castle. Folktales and legends remain woven around the castle's ruins—chew them over at the famous farmhouse restaurant halfway up.

Castle in the air As locations for defensive castles go, they don't come much better than Castell d'Alaró's spectacular mountaintop. The Moors were the first to spot its potential, at the entrance to the Tramuntana mountains, and built a fort that withstood a two-year siege during the Christian conquest of Mallorca. But Castell d'Alaró's fame rests on another incident. In 1285, as King Alfonso III marched across the island he met fierce resistance at Castell d'Alaró, whose commanders stayed loyal to Jaume II.

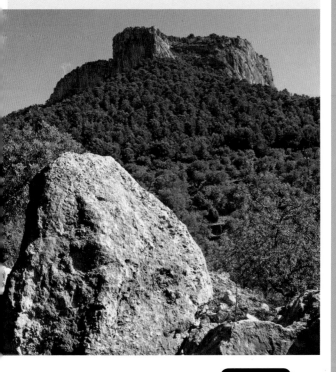

From left to right: The centuries-old route up to Castel d'Alaró; an archway at Castel d'Alaró; the perfect defensive position

As the king of Aragon attempted to take the castle, a sentry named Cabrit called out: 'We like our *anfós* [fish] grilled!' King Alfonso replied: 'And I like my *cabrit* [goat] roasted!' Sadly for the sentry, Alfonso was true to his word when the castle was breached and he burned the impudent sentry alive on a spit.

Walk this way Legends aside, Castell d'Alaró is a spectacular day trip. You can drive halfway up the mountain and park at Es Verger, a rustic res-taurant, but the unpaved track is very narrow and rocky and meeting other cars can be a problem. An alternative for the fit is to walk up. At the top, beyond the castle ruins, 800m (2,625ft) above sea level is a small chapel and sanctuary, Nostra Senyora del Refugio; it's simple, beautiful and you can stay the night in the hostel if need be.

Deià

Honey-stone houses surrounded by mountains to one side and the sparkling Mediterranean on the other; it isn't hard to see what drew writer Robert Graves and subsequent artists and celebrities to this picturesque village.

Delightful Deià 'The mountains rise up on every side, enclosing the sloping town and its hill in a warm and perfumed hollow.' Gordon West's description of Deià in the 1920s still applies today: strict planning laws mean that the village's houses are as beautiful as ever; the only difference is that they are owned by millionaires today rather than Mallorcans.

Poet's haven Since the 1940s, Deià's most famous residents have been the Graves family.

Clockwise from left: The town of Deià blends into the surrounding countryside; the main square of Deià is quiet and picturesque; typical shuttered window in the town; Ca's Xorc is a hotel with stunning views of the countryside near Deià

Poet Robert Graves lived in the house Ca n'Alluny from 1946 until his death in 1985, attracting a stream of artists and writers to the town, including Ava Gardner, Anaïs Nin and Kingsley Amis. His son, William, has turned the house into a museum. A tour of the house reveals Graves' own writing desk and, most excitingly, his own printing press. His kitchen, dining room, study and bedroom and their 1950s furnishings are all intact. Graves is buried in the small cemetery beside the church of Sant Joan Baptista, reached by climbing the Carrer d'es Puig.

Local hero Ca n'Alluny isn't the only attraction in Deià; the museum Son Marroig (▷ 71) is dedicated to the life of the Archduke Luis Salvador, while Mallorcan history goes even further back in Deià's own Archaeological Museum.

THE BASICS

🔹 D4
🚌 Bus 210 from Palma, Sóller and Valldemossa
❓ Classical music festival Aug–Sep

Ca n'Alluny
www.fundaciorobertgraves.com
✉ Carretera de Sóller
☎ 971 636 185
🕐 Apr–Oct Mon–Fri 10–5, Sat 10–3; Nov Mon–Fri 9–2; Dec–Mar Mon–Fri 10.30–1.30
💰 Moderate

61

Monastir de Lluc

On a devoutly Catholic island, Mallorca's largest and best-known monastery and its museum is the focal point for locals and many more pilgrims, although its remote, beautiful location is equally appealing as the basilica.

A monk's tale The monastery at Lluc is the most sacred site on Mallorca. According to local legend it has been a place of pilgrimage since the 13th century, when an Arab shepherd boy found a wooden statue of the Virgin that had been hidden in a cave at Lluc during the Moorish rule. A chapel was built to house the statue; within years miracles were being attributed to the statue.

Mary's statue Today, Lluc monastery is much expanded: the complex comprises a basilica with

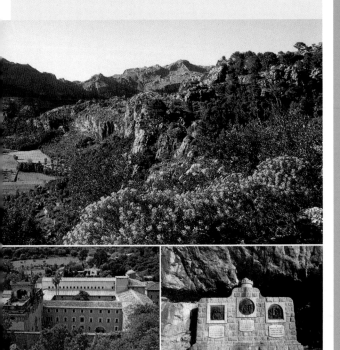

a baroque façade dating from 1622, a botanical garden used to grow medicinal herbs and the Museu de Lluc. Your first stop should be the basilica itself, reached via the courtyard inside the main complex. Inside the basilica stands an object of veneration for many people: La Moreneta (The Little Dark One). This small statue of the Virgin wears a gift from the people of Mallorca in 1884: a crown of precious gems. When the devout have paid their respects to La Moreneta they will make their way to Mass, held daily at 11am.

Pilgrim's progress Once out of the basilica, don't miss the Way of the Rosary, a path to the left of the monastery complex lined with granite monuments representing the Stations of the Cross. The 10-minute walk to the summit leads to a replacement wooden cross.

THE BASICS

➕ G3

✉ Carretera Ma-2140

☎ 971 871 525

🕐 Museum: daily 10–1.30, 2.30–5.15; monastery: daily 9–8.30

💷 Museum: inexpensive; monastery: free

🚌 Buses from Palma via Inca, Pollença and Sóller.

🍽 Café Sa Fonda (€–€€)

❓ The choir sings daily at the 11am Mass

Pollença and Port de Pollença

HIGHLIGHT

● Climb the 365 steps to the chapel of Calvary in Pollença. The chapel, dating from 1799, contains a 14th-century carving of the Mother of God at the Foot of the Cross.

TIP

● There are strict parking regulations in Port de Pollença. But you can park more easily further away from the centre and walk in along the path around the bay.

Stylish Pollença and its port are popular bases for a largely British clientele. The town has lots to see and do while the port offers an attractive promenade, watersports and sunbathing potential.

Easy-going but elegant Pollença, with an enviable location at the tip of the Tramuntana, has retained an air of tranquillity despite its popularity as a base for mainly British holiday-makers. It's a pretty town with a good range of shops and restaurants—but all still affordable and laid-back. In short, it has found a happy balance between exclusivity and accessibility. Pollença is very much a working town and life revolves around the Plaça Major, which is surrounded by several cafés from where locals and visitors watch the world go by. From the solid-looking

Clockwise from left: Descending the Calvary steps; some of the streets in Pollença are just steep steps; night-time in Pollença's Plaça Major; the Pont Roma (Roman Bridge) spans a dry riverbed near Pollença; watersports at Port de Pollença; the view from Mirador des Colomer over the Tramuntana to Port de Pollença in the distance

town hall, once a Jesuit convent, follow a flight of 365 steps up to the Calvary chapel.

The town's story There are two museums in the town: the Museu Martí Vicenç, a museum of textiles, and the Museu de Pollença, which has a collection of art and items related to the town.

The port's resort Many Mallorcan towns were built some distance from their ports and Pollença is no exception; it is a 10-minute drive to Port de Pollença and the sea. Occupying one side of a bay, Port de Pollença is an almost genteel resort with a mediocre beach but plenty of charm to make up for it. Explore the seafront on foot, following the pine-scented path to the historic Illa d'Or hotel (▷ 112). It's a family-friendly town with lots of activities taking place in the bay.

THE BASICS

🚩 H2

ℹ️ Passeig Saralegui, s/n, Port de Pollença, tel 971 865 467

🚌 Buses from Alcúdia and Palma

Museu Martí Vicenç
www.martivicens.org
✉️ Carrer del Calvari, 10
☎️ 971 532 867

Museu de Pollença
www.ajpollenca.net
✉️ Carrer Guillem Cifre de Colonya ☎️ 971 531 166

Sóller and Port de Sóller

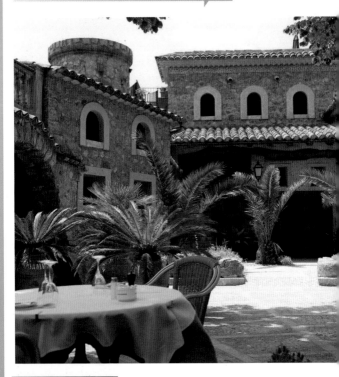

HIGHLIGHTS

● Sóller is a place to potter; there are few tour buses so take time to sip a freshly squeezed orange juice in Plaça Constitució and relax.
● The port is the perfect spot to see the sunset.

TIPS

● Take the tram from Sóller to the port.
● Tunnels through the mountains between Sóller and Palma mean that road access is quick and easy.

At the heart of the Sóller valley in the Tramuntana mountains, the busy town of Sóller offers access to the compact port and marina via a tram.

Oranges and lemons The largest town in the Tramuntana is a superb base for exploring the central stretch of the mountain range. Deià, Lluc and Valldemossa are just a short drive away and there are two lovely mountain villages nearby: Biniaraix and Fornalutx. Sóller occupies a wide valley filled with citrus groves providing fresh fruit all year round. These harvests made Sóller rich and the town has some ornate Modernist architecture as a result: look for the Modernist window grilles at the Banco Central Hispano and the façade of the church of Sant Bartomeu in the Plaça Constitució, the town's main square. From

Clockwise from left: Sóller's Ca n'Aí is a hotel that has been owned by the same family for 14 generations; Port de Sóller viewed from Mirador de ses Barques; detail of the exterior of the Banco Central Hispano

THE BASICS

www.sollernet.com

✚ E3

ℹ Plaça Espanya, tel 971 638 008

🚌 Buses from Palma and Valldemossa; tram from Sóller to Port de Sóller

🚊 Train from Palma via Bunyola

Museu de Sóller

✉ Carrer de Sa Mar, 13, Sóller

☎ 971 631 465

🕐 Mon–Fri 11–4, Sat 11–1

Can Prunera

www.canprunera.com

✉ Carrer Sa Lluna, 86–90

☎ 971 638 973

🕐 Mar–Oct daily 10.30–6.30; Nov–Feb Tue–Sun 10.30–6

Jardí Botanic

✉ Ctra. Palma-Port de Sóller km 30.5, Sóller

☎ 971 634 014

🕐 Mar–Oct Mon–Sat 10–6; Nov, Jan–Feb Thu–Sat 10–2. Closed Dec.

this square follow Carrer Sa Lluna, the town's best shopping street.

Petite port The town's main sights include the Museu de Sóller, the natural science museum (Museu Balear de Ciencies Naturals) and an excellent art museum, Can Prunera, with paintings by Picasso, Matisse, Léger and Miró. There is also a delightful botanical garden, the Jardí Botanic. A tram links Sóller with its port, the sedate resort of Port de Sóller, where numerous restaurants and some bars line the seafront. The tiny port is surrounded on three sides by steep mountains with a narrow entrance to the bay.

Walking away Sóller is near the Tramuntana's walking routes and a walkers' refuge, La Muleta, is just above the port, next to the lighthouse.

Valldemossa

TOP
25

HIGHLIGHTS

● The annual Chopin festival
is in August, and there is also
music from other composers
(www.festivalchopin.com).
● The ivory triptych in the
Reial Cartoixa's library.

TIP

● Avoid the tour groups by
arriving early or late.

**Frédéric Chopin, who wintered here,
spurred Valldemossa's rise to the top of
sightseers' lists, but the handsome town
would have found popularity regardless,
thanks to an influential monastery and
some important attractions.**

Musical interlude When Frédéric Chopin and
his mistress George Sand were looking for some-
where to recuperate during the winter of 1838–
39 little did they know that their short stay would
spur Valldemossa's tourism boom more than a
century later. But the town, Mallorca's highest,
has plenty to see beyond the Chopin connection.
Chopin and Sand rented rooms in Valldemossa's
monastery, the Reial Cartoixa (he composed
piano pieces on the rickety instrument in Cell
4). The Reial Cartoixa was founded in 1835 by

Clockwise from top left: Flower-filled pots in a side street of Valldemossa; church interior in the Reial Cartoixa; Valldemossa is a jumble of houses and monastic buildings; majolica plates for sale; a tile showing Mallorca's patron saint, Catalina Thomás; Valldemossa's open-air market

Carthusian monks but is now in private hands. You can still get a feel for monastic life on the tour of the church, cloisters and cells, however it can be very busy. Next to the Reial Cartoixa, the Palau del Reii Sanc is included in the entry fee but the highlight is the view from the terrace.

Inspiring setting Also in the monastery's main building, Valldemossa's Museu Municipal introduces some of the artists inspired by the surrounding Mallorcan mountains, including the town's most famous artist, Josep Coll Bardolet (1912–2007). A modern gallery in central Valldemossa, the Fundació Cultural Coll Bardolet, is dedicated to his work. There are activities here during the summer season, plus temporary exhibitions. It is a great place to see the landscapes of the Tramuntana through a local's eyes.

THE BASICS

www.valldemossa.com
🔹 D4
🔹 Avinguda de Palma, 7, tel 971 612 019
🚌 From Palma and Sóller

Reial Cartoixa
www.cartujadevalldemossa.com
✉ Plaça Cartoixa
☎ 971 612 106
🕐 Apr–Sep Mon–Sat 9.30–6.30, Sun 10–1; Mar, Oct Mon–Sat 9.30–5.30; Nov–Feb Mon–Sat 9.30–3
🖐 Moderate

Fundació Cultural Coll Bardolet
www.fccollbardolet.org
✉ Carrer Blanquerna, 4
☎ 971 612 983
🕐 Apr–Oct Mon–Sat 10–2, 3–7, Sun and hols 10–2, 4–8; Nov–Mar Mon–Sat 10–4, Sun and hols 10–2, 3–6

More to See

CALA SANT VICENÇ

At the northern tip of the Tramuntana range, this traditional resort is more fashionable than most, with chic hotels and restaurants. Based around a series of four small coves, each with a tiny beach, Cala Sant Vicenç attracts locals at the weekends. You can walk there from Port de Pollença.

H2 Plaça Sant Vicenç, tel 971 533 264 Good seafood restaurants

COSTA NORD

www.costanord.es

This cultural centre in Valldemossa hosts a range of activities including film screenings and guided walks. But its most notable event is the month-long Mediterranean Nights series of concerts during the summer. The centre, once owned by actor Michael Douglas, was opened in 2000 and retains close links with him—Douglas has said that Costa Nord is his personal tribute to the island.

D4 Avinguda de Palma, 6, Valldemossa 971 612 425 Daily 9–5 Moderate

FORNALUTX

If you leave Sóller and head towards Lluc you will pass this pretty mountain village. Thanks to narrow roads it suffers from congestion but once you've settled on a sunny terrace it doesn't seem to matter. There are several good traditional restaurants here and the views across the valley are mesmerizing. Neighbouring Biniaraix vies with Fornalutx for accolades but is not as high.

E3 Several good traditional restaurants

JARDINES D'ALFABIA

www.jardinesdealfabia.com

When the Moors arrived on Mallorca they created this estate in the foothills of the Tramuntana. In the 18th century the Mallorcan owners planted tropical gardens that, in the words of one observer, seemed to merge with the mountains. Take time to wander through the walkways and water gardens and explore the shady corners and grand house.

E4 Carretera de Sóller, km17, Bunyola

The steep narrow pathways of Fornalutx

Don't miss the colourful Jardines d'Alfabia

☎ 971 613 123 ⏰ Apr–Oct Mon–Sat 9.30–
6.30; Nov Mar Mon–Fri 9.30–5.30, Sat 9.30–1
💷 Inexpensive 🚆 The train station at nearby
Bunyola is on the Palma–Sóller line

ORIENT
The minuscule village of Orient
is tucked into a very pretty corner
of Mallorca, where the vineyards
and olive groves of the lowlands
meet the craggy slopes of the
Tramuntana. To get here you'll have
to take it slowly as the road twists
through forests of stunted, gnarled
trees. Walkers will be delighted:
lots of trails can be followed into
the hills, including one route up to
Castell d'Alaró (▷ 58–59) from the
Hotel Hermitage.
➕ E4 🍴 Limited restaurants and cafés

SA CALOBRA
More challenging driving awaits at
the junction of the Sóller to Lluc
road with the road down to this
cove. The road twists and turns
down the 800m (2,600ft) cliff-side;
an alternative during the summer is
to take a boat from Port de Sóller.
Once at Sa Calobra, expect to share
this photogenic cove with other
sightseers. Follow the paths to Cala
Tuent, a sandy cove with a small
church, or the Torrent de Pareis, a
splendid precipitous gorge, but note
that you won't have it to yourself.
➕ F2 🍴 Restaurants 🚢 From Port de
Sóller (Barcos Azules, ▷ 75)

SON MARROIG
www.sonmarroig.com
The Archduke Ludwig Salvador was
one of Mallorca's earliest and most-
loved expat residents. With a strong
conservation ethos and deep pock-
ets, he bought numerous estates
around the island and the stately
home, Son Marroig, is a museum
of the Archduke's life and work. The
highlight is the view of Sa Foradada,
a hole in the rocky peninsula visible
from the garden's marble rotunda.
➕ D3 ✉ Carretera Valldemossa–Deià
☎ 971 639 158 ⏰ Mon–Thu 9–1,
Fri, Sat 9–5. Closed Sun 💷 Moderate
🍴 Restaurant and café (€)

*The countryside near Orient is excellent for
walking*

*A view of Son Marroig through the slender
pillars of the Carrara marble belvedere*

Camels and Choirboys

Behind Lluc Monastery, this path used by wild goats leads to soaring mountain vistas, a witch's nest and a rock shaped like a camel.

DISTANCE: 3.2km (2 miles) **ALLOW:** 2 hours

START .... **END**

MONASTIR DE LLUC
🚩 G3 🚌 Buses from Palma via Inca, Pollença and Sóller

MONASTIR DE LLUC

1 Using the gravel pavement, follow the main road out of Lluc Monastery. Take the next left turn, marked Camí Reservat, and then take the immediate right after the gateposts, signposted Es Camell.

7 Take the right turn at a wooden gate, marked by a spot of red paint. Follow the path, once a 13th-century highway, downhill back to the football pitch from where you can return to the monastery car park.

6 Turn right, taking care beside the fast road (walk high up the verge). Go past a driveway to Binifaldó.

2 You'll arrive at a football pitch used by the choristers at the monastery's school; cross it diagonally and leave by the gate in the far left corner. Cross the footbridge across the Torrent de Lluc, which is anything but a torrent for most of the year.

5 Turn around and follow the wide path back past the junction and tree with growth that has been nicknamed 'the witch's nest'. The path climbs up beside old stone walls until it reaches the Sóller–Lluc road.

3 At the boulder field, follow the worn boulders up to the left. At the top there is a flattened area of ground, site of a charcoal burners' camp. An easy-to-miss path to the right leads to Camel Rock, some 50m (55 yards) away.

4 Retrace your steps to the main path and turn right, climbing up a gradual slope to a junction. To the left the broad trail leads to a viewpoint, the Mirador des Pixarells, with benches looking out over the limestone mountains.

From Sóller to Pollença

The spectacular Ma-10 road runs through the mountains from the Sóller valley almost to the sea.

DISTANCE: 56km (34 miles) **ALLOW:** 3–4 hours with stops
(traffic is busy and slow in summer)

START

THE EASTERN JUNCTION OF THE MA-10 WITH THE ROAD FROM SÓLLER TO PORT DE SÓLLER, SIGNPOSTED LLUC
✚ E3 🚌 L210, L211, L212

1 The road from Sóller to Lluc begins at a roundabout just outside Sóller (on the port side). Follow the wide road uphill. Halfway up the meandering road a turning to the right leads to Biniaraix and Fornalutx, two of the prettiest villages in the Tramuntana.

2 There are several traditional restaurants in Fornalutx where you can stop for lunch, otherwise continue up the Ma-10. At the top there is a viewpoint just before the first tunnel through the mountains overlooking the Sóller valley.

3 After the tunnel, the road winds around the edge of the Embassament de Cúber (the Cúber dam), with Puig Major, Mallorca's highest mountain, looming on the left. This is the territory of the black vulture, Europe's largest and rarest bird of prey.

END

POLLENÇA
✚ H2 🚌 L340

6 This stretch of the drive passes through forests of gnarled pine trees before opening out into a rocky landscape. The road descends into Pollença via the west side of town. You can park in the residential streets before walking into the town centre.

5 The road twists through mountain scenery before Lluc is signposted to the left. Bear left and stay on the road, signposted Pollença.

4 The road runs alongside the Embassament de Gorg Blau before starting to climb again towards a left turn to Sa Calobra (▷ 71). You can take the diversion down to sea level again but the narrow road is exceptionally congested in summer. Otherwise continue on towards Lluc monastery.

Shopping

BENNASSAR GALERIES

www.galeriesbennassar.com
Named after a Mallorcan artist, this gallery sells original paintings from a range of artists.

🔟 H2 ⊠ Plaça Major, 6, Pollença ☎ 971 533 514 🕐 Thu–Sat 10–1.30, 5–8.30, Sun 11–1.30

BESTARD

www.bestard.com
World-class walking boots are made here in the factory founded in 1940.

🔟 F4 ⊠ Carrer Estació, 40–42, Lloseta ☎ 971 514 044 🕐 Mon–Sat 10.30–2.30, 5–9.30, Sun 10.30–3

BISANYES

Possibly the best bakery in town with savoury goodies, tasty breads and sweet treats to take away.

🔟 H2 ⊠ Avinguda de Juan XXIII, 125, Port de Pollença ☎ 971 867 016 🕐 Mon–Sat 8–6, Sun 8–2

SA FABRICA DE GELATS

www.gelatsoller.com
Out-of-this-world, artisan ice cream made in Sóller.

🔟 E3 ⊠ Plaça del Mercat, Sóller ☎ 971 631 708 🕐 Daily 10–2, 4–8

FET A SÓLLER

www.fetasoller.com
Selling locally produced ceramics, *sobrassada* (spicy sausage), olive oil and preserves.

🔟 E3 ⊠ Carrer Romaguera, 12, Sóller ☎ 971 638 839 🕐 Mon–Sat 9–7

GALERIA MAIOR

www.galeriamaior.com
This large space for contemporary art includes paintings, installations and sculpture. There's a sister gallery in Palma.

🔟 H2 ⊠ Plaça Major, 4, Pollença ☎ 971 530 095 🕐 Tue–Fri 10.30–1.30, 5–8; Sat 10.30–1.30, Sun 11–1.30

LAFIORE

www.lafiore.com
Technicolour glass creations by Mallorca's famed glass blowers—see a demonstration here.

🔟 D4 ⊠ Carretera Valldemossa, S'Esgleieta, Esporles ☎ 971 611 800 🕐 Mon–Fri 9.15–8, Sat 9–2, 3–6

OLI CAIMARI

www.aceites-olicaimari.com
One of the island's largest olive oil producers has an outlet just outside Caimari with a variety of oils and other Mallorcan products.

BUYING LOCAL

The spirit of independence remains strong on Mallorca and opportunities to support local businesses aren't lacking. In the Serra de Tramuntana you can buy food products, cosmetics, clothes and footwear, jewellery, souvenirs and even art produced by locals. Visitors get an authentically Mallorcan product and the income stays in the local economy.

🔟 G3 ⊠ Carretera Inca–Lluc, km6, Caimari ☎ 971 873 577 🕐 Mon–Fri 9–7, Sat 10–2, 4–7, Sun 10–2

PORENT

There's no shortage of souvenir shops in Valldemossa but this one stocks an interesting range of Mallorcan handicrafts (olive wood, tiles) and a range of gourmet foods (Frasquet artisan chocolate, Mallorcan olive oil).

🔟 D4 ⊠ Carrer Blanquerna, 6, Valldemossa ☎ 971 612 379 🕐 Daily 11–6 (7 in summer)

SHOBHA DIANE

www.shobha-diane.com
This jewellery shop in Pollença sells startling and original pieces. It specializes in chunky amber jewellery, but can custom-make items to your design.

🔟 H2 ⊠ Carrer Temple, 6, Pollença ☎ 971 534 466 🕐 Daily 11–2, 6–8.30; closed Wed am, Sat and Sun pm, winter pm

THINK COSMETIC

www.thinkcosmetic.com
Innovative cosmetics company making body and haircare products from natural ingredients such as yoghurt, honey, almond, sea fennel and carob. Available here in Pollença and also stocked at many of the area's hotels.

🔟 H2 ⊠ Carrer Calvari, 1, Pollença ☎ 971 533 085 🕐 Sun–Fri 10–2, 4–7.30

Entertainment and Activities

BARCOS AZULES
www.barcosazules.com
A long-established, family-run business, Barcos Azules operates regular boat trips from Port de Sóller to Sa Calobra (▷ 71), Cala Tuent, Cap de Formentor (▷ 56–57) and even Menorca.
✚ E3 ✉ Passeig Es Través, 3, Port de Sóller ☎ 971 630 170

EL BARRIGON XELINI
www.xelini.com
This airy tapas bar has a counter with market-fresh tapas dishes (including sardines and cured hams) and a bar stocked with the traditional tapas accompaniments of fino sherry, beer or wine. As well as the bar area, there's an outdoor terrace and restaurant seating.
✚ D4 ✉ Carrer Archiduque Luis Salvador, 19, Deià ☎ 971 639 139 🕐 Tue–Sun 12.30–12.30 (11.30 in winter)

MANDUCA
Buzzing pizzeria and bar with outside seating and drinks offers.
✚ H2 ✉ Econom Torres, 11, Port de Pollença ☎ 971 866 609 🕐 Daily 1–4, 7–11.30

REIAL CLUB NÁUTICO PORT DE POLLENÇA
www.rcnpp.net
Port de Pollença's yacht club offers sailing lessons and a good range of other watersports from its base on the bay.
✚ H2 ✉ Moll Vell, Port de Pollença ☎ 971 864 635

RENT MARCH
www.rentmarch.com
This is a handy place to rent a bike, scooter or even a tandem; prices are reasonable and the bicycles are kept in excellent condition.
✚ H2 ✉ Avinguda de Juan XIII, 9, Port de Pollença ☎ 971 864 784

RUTA DE PEDRA EN SEC
The 150km (93-mile) Dry-Stone Route in the Tramuntana mountains can be broken into eight stages so you can walk as much or as little of it as you like. There are several *refuges* where you can spend the night. Contact the Consell de Mallorca,

FESTIVALS
If you're in Pollença during July and August try to catch a performance during the annual Classical Music Festival, which has taken place in the town since 1961. It is based at the 17th-century cloisters of Sant Domingo, where open-air performances (weather permitting) start at 10pm. Concerts at the world-class event may include gospel, classical Spanish guiter, concert pianists and orchestras. There are further summer music festivals at Costa Nord (▷ 70) and Son Marroig (▷ 71).
✚ H2 ☎ 971 534 011; www.festivalpollenca.org.

tel: 971 173 700, for maps and reservations.
Refugi Muleta ✚ E3 ✉ Far de Cap Gros, Port de Sóller 🍴 Food available on site
Tossals Verds ✚ F3 ✉ Escorca, Finca Tossals Verd (near Cúber Reservoir) 🍴 Food available on site
Can Boi ✚ D4 ✉ Carrer des Clots, 5, Deià 🍴 Food available on site

SCUBA MALLORCA
www.scubamallorca.com
Learn to scuba dive with this PADI-accredited company or join trips out to Cap de Formentor and around the bay. Hotel pick-ups can be arranged.
✚ H2 ✉ Carrer d'El Cano, 23, Port de Pollença ☎ 971 868 087 🕐 Mar to mid-Nov

TEATRE LLOSETA
www.teatrelloseta.com
This modern theatre has music, drama and dance performances plus book readings and exhibitions.
✚ F4 ✉ Carrer Pou Nou, Lloseta ☎ 971 514 452 🕐 Variable

TRAMUNTANA TOURS
www.tramuntanatours.com
Rent a bike and explore the Serra de Tramuntana or join a bike tour. Other adventure activities include canyoning, fishing and sea kayaking. A second office opens in Port de Sóller in the summer.
✚ E3 ✉ Calle de la Luna, 72, Sóller ☎ 971 632 423 🕐 Mon–Fri 9–1.30, 3–7.30, Sat 9–1.30

Restaurants

PRICES

Prices are approximate, based on a 3-course meal for one person.
€€€   over €40
€€   €20–€40
€   under €20

BÉNS D'AVALL (€€€)

www.benetvicens.com
Owner Benet Vicens ensures fresh, seasonal ingredients for his Modern Mallorcan cuisine at one of the island's best restaurants.

➕ D3 ✉ Carretera Sóller–Deià ☎ 971 632 381 ⏰ Daily lunch and dinner; closed Mon and Tue Oct–Mar

CA N'ANTUNA (€–€€)

Famed throughout the Tramuntana for its slow-roasted suckling pig and shoulder of lamb. A shaded terrace has views over the Sóller valley. Service is brusque but efficient.

➕ E3 ✉ Carrer Arbona Colom, 8, Fornalutx ☎ 971 633 068 ⏰ Tue–Sun lunch and dinner

ES FARO (€€€)

www.restaurantesfaro.es
Enjoy pretty views of Port de Sóller from the windows of Es Faro, up near the lighthouse overlooking the port. Like the location, prices for the seafood are high but the views are worth it (and the drive or walk up).

➕ E3 ✉ Cap Gros de Moleta, Port de Sóller ☎ 971 633 752 ⏰ Daily lunch and dinner

LA FONDA (€–€€)

Traditional, seasonal Mallorcan cooking adjacent to Pollença's Plaça Major. The *menú del dia* is excellent value.

➕ H2 ✉ Carrer Antoni Maura, 32, Pollença ☎ 971 534 751 ⏰ Tue–Sun lunch and dinner

EL OLIVO (€€€)

www.hotel-laresidencia.com
With a heavenly setting overlooking Deià, a modern Mediterranean menu and a superb best wine list, El Olivo is a good choice for a special-occasion meal.

➕ D4 ✉ Hotel La Residencia, Son Canals, Deià ☎ 971 639 011 ⏰ Daily lunch and dinner

LA TERRASSA (€€–€€€)

www.hotelillador.com
At the Formentor end of the bay of Pollença, the restaurant of the Illa d'Or hotel has a sun-drenched terrace and an airy interior with views across the bay. The Mediterranean-influenced menu has fish dishes and salads. Superb service.

➕ H2 ✉ Hotel Illa d'Or, Passeig Colón, 265, Port de Pollença ☎ 971 865 100 ⏰ Feb–Nov daily lunch and dinner

ES VERGER (€–€€)

Grab a space on the benches in this rustic restaurant halfway up the mountain. At €16 for shoulder of lamb and suckling pig, it's one of Mallorca's quintessential dining treats.

➕ F4 ✉ Castell d'Alaró ☎ 971 182 126 ⏰ Tue–Sat lunch and dinner, Sun lunch

SA VINYA (€€–€€€)

www.restaurant-savinya.com
Head for a table on Sa Vinya's terrace and enjoy glorious views of the mountains. The food is light and delicious: choose from the likes of gazpacho with melon and tarragon, sea bass with chorizo couscous, or a tasty meat or fish risotto, followed by one of the delicious homemade desserts. Service can be a little haphazard but the stunning surroundings more than compensate for this. Reservations are recommended.

➕ D4 ✉ Carrer Viña Vieja, Deià ☎ 971 639 500 ⏰ Feb–Nov Wed–Mon 1–11

EATING OUT

Restaurants in the Tramuntana are divided between nourishing walkers who march in off the mountains with large appetites and delighting the day-tripping foodies who make the trip up from Palma to visit some of Mallorca's most exclusive restaurants. The restaurant guide on page 15 will tell you which restaurants offer filling but rustic courses and which serve daintier modern Mallorcan meals.

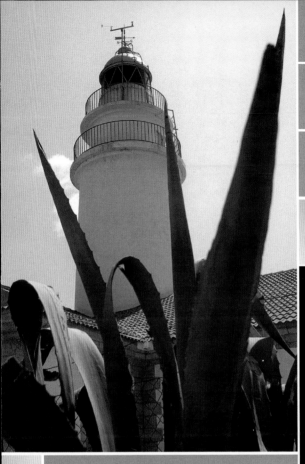

The Northeast of Mallorca sees the foothills of the Tramuntana subside into the bird-rich marshes of S'Albufera and the fertile fields of Es Pla. This area is rich in history but beachlife is also an attraction, with some of Mallorca's largest resorts and some of its most secluded beaches.

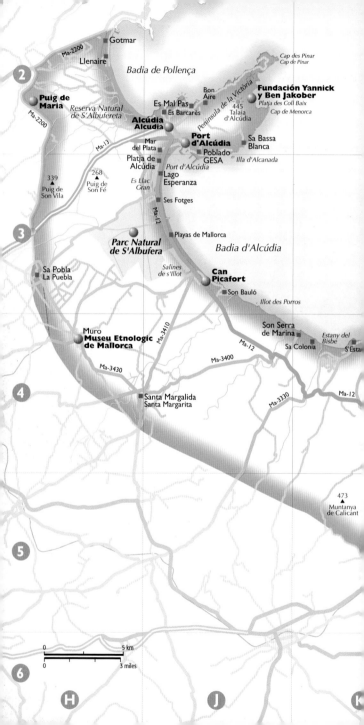

Gotmar

Ma-2200

Llenaire

Badia de Pollença

Cap des Pinar
Cap de Pinar

Bon
Aire

Es Mal Pas

**Fundación Yannick
y Ben Jakober**

Platja des Coll Baix

**Puig de
Maria**

*Reserva Natural
de S'Albufereta*

Es Barcarès

445
Talaia
d'Alcúdia

Cap de Menorca

Ma-2200

Alcúdia
Alcudia

Ma-13

Mar
del Plata

**Port
d'Alcúdia**

Sa Bassa
Blanca

Platja de
Alcúdia

Port d'Alcúdia

Poblado
GESA

339
▲
Puig de
Son Vila

268
▲
Puig de
Son Fé

Lago
Esperanza

Illa d'Alcanada

*Es Llac
Gran*

Ma-12

Ses Fotges

Playas de Mallorca

Badia d'Alcúdia

**Parc Natural
de S'Albufera**

*Salines
de s'Illot*

**Can
Picafort**

Sa Pobla
La Puebla

Son Bauló

Illot des Porros

Muro
**Museu Etnologic
de Mallorca**

Ma-3410

Son Serra
de Marina

*Estany del
Bisbe*

Ma-12

Sa Colonia

S'Esta

Ma-3400

Ma-3430

Santa Margalida
Santa Margarita

Ma-3330

Ma-12

473
▲
Muntanya
de Calicant

0   5 km

0   3 miles

H   **J**   **K**

2

3

4

5

6

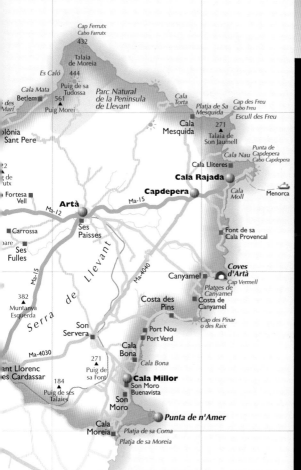

Cap Ferrutx
Cabo Farrutx
432

Talaia
de Moreia
444

Es Caló

Cala Mata
Betlem
Puig de sa
Tudossa
561
Puig Morei

Parc Natural
de la Península
de Llevant

Cala
Torta

Platja de Sa
Mesquida
Cap des Freu
Cabo Freu
Escull des Freu

des
Mari

Cala
Mesquida

Cala
Mesquida

Talaia de
Son Jaumell
271

Punta de
Capdepera
Cabo Capdepera

olònia
Sant Pere

Cala Nau

Cala Lliteres

Cala Rajada

2
de
utx

Fortesa
Vell

Artà

Ma-12

Ma-15

Capdepera

Cala
Moll

Menorca

Carrossa

Ses
Paisses

Font de sa
Cala Provençal

pare
Ses
Fulles

Ma-15

*Coves
d'Artà*

Cap Vermell

382
Muntanya
Esquerda

Ma-4040

Canyamel

Platges de
Canyamel

Costa de
Canyamel

Costa des
Pins

Cap des Pinar
o des Raix

Son
Servera

Ma-4030

Port Nou
Port Verd

271
Puig de
sa Font

Cala
Bona

Cala Bona

ant Llorenç
es Cardassar

184
Puig de ses
Talaies

Cala Millor
Son Moro
Buenavista

Son
Moro

Punta de n'Amer

Cala
Moreia

Platja de sa Coma

Platja de sa Moreia

Serra   de   Llevant

Ⓛ   Ⓜ

Alcúdia and Port d'Alcúdia

● The Museu Monografic de Pollentia displays many of the finds from Alcúdia's Roman ruins, including coins, toys and a 2nd-century bronze head of a girl.

TIP

● Take time to explore the Peninsula de la Victòria; its rugged slopes have a variety of walking tracks and one of Mallorca's best art galleries, the Fundación Yannick y Ben Jakober (▷ 82–83).

The historic town of Alcúdia has the best-preserved old quarter in Mallorca with rock-solid walls and even Roman ruins. Sunseekers will want to continue to Port d'Alcúdia where lengthy beaches are backed by busy resorts.

Roam a Roman world Rather confusingly, Pollentia is the name of the Roman ruins that lie just outside Alcúdia's city walls. These ruins consist of a first-century theatre, hewn out of the rock, a forum and La Portella, the remains of a residential district. The entire site is the most significant evidence of Roman civilization in the Balearics and is accessible and cheap to visit.

Ancient and modern Alcúdia occupies a strategic position on the north coast between two

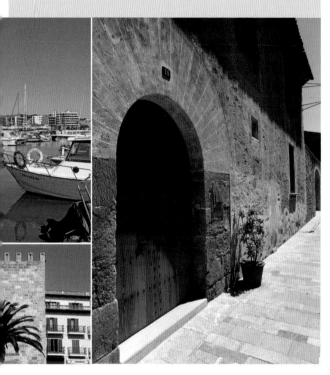

Clockwise from left: Roman ruins at Pollentia, near Alcúdia; boats in the harbour at Alcúdia; Can Tem is a hotel in the medieval centre of Alcúdia; the entrance to the medieval town

bays and it wasn't just the Romans who recognized its value: the city was conquered by Moors, Byzantines and Christians, who, in the 14th century, began the immense medieval walls and fortified gates you can see today. Inside the 1.6km (1-mile) restored perimeter wall, the old town of Alcúdia has several boutique hotels and if you stick to the old town and follow the walls it's an interesting maze to explore on foot.

Last resort Alcúdia has been superseded, however, by its port. From Port d'Alcúdia resort hotels march east along Mallorca's largest bay all the way to Can Picafort. This is summer-holiday territory, with beaches glistening with northern Europeans. The upside to this is the variety of activities on offer but the area does close down in the winter.

THE BASICS

➕ J2
ℹ️ Alcúdia: Carrer Major 17, tel 971 897 100
ℹ️ Port d'Alcúdia: Passeig Marítim, tel 971 547 257

Museu Monografic de Pollentia
✉️ Carrer Sant Jaume 30, Alcúdia
☎️ 971 547 004
🕐 Tue–Sun 10–12, 4–6
💷 Moderate

Fundación Yannick y Ben Jakober

The fundación has a variety of exhibition spaces inside and out

THE BASICS

J2
www.fundacionjakober.org
✉ Finca Sa Bassa Blanca, Camí del Coll Baix, Mal Pas, Alcúdia
☎ 971 549 880
🕐 Open day: Tue 9.30–12.30, 2.30–5.30. Tours by appointment: Wed–Sat
♿ Variable, some parts of gallery free on Tue

HIGHLIGHT

● The Nins gallery has more than 150 portraits of children painted from the 16th to 19th centuries. It is an artistically and historically important collection.

TIP

● For visits on days other than Tuesday, entrance fees are charged per exhibition. A whole-day voucher gives access to all exhibitions and is the most cost-effective option.

With a sculpture park, rose garden, a gallery of classical portraits of children and a house full of modern art, this is a remarkable arts foundation and one of Mallorca's best-kept secrets.

Eccentric and eclectic It's hard to find, at the end of an unpaved road on the Peninsula de la Victòria beyond Alcúdia, but the drive is worth it. Founded by Ben Jakober and Yannick Vu, a couple at the heart of Europe's contemporary arts scene, the galleries and gardens at Sa Bassa Blanca will take half a day to explore. Yannick and Ben prefer to think of the artworks they have amassed as a record of friendships and collaborations rather than an art collection.

Euro art There are several distinct parts of the foundation. The main house has a mix of Moorish decorative work, such as a glorious Mudejar ceiling, and contemporary sculpture and painting. In Room 1 the British artist Rebecca Horn has loaned her *Dreaming Stones* installation, which uses movement sensors to trigger its action. The next room is dedicated to the Italian painter Domenico Gnoli (Yannick's first husband), who contributed *What Is A Monster?* to Robert Graves' *A Modern Bestiary*.

Sculpture garden Outside, don't miss the walled rose garden, which blooms in May. An avenue lined with sculptures, which children will love, leads to the underground SoKra TES space with a skeleton of a Woolly Rhinoceros as its centrepiece.

Artà

From left: Approaching
Artà; Santuari de Sant
Salvador; exterior of
the sanctuary

THE BASICS

L4

Santuari de Sant Salvador
☎ 971 836 136
🕐 Daily 8–6

Ses Països
✉ Camí de sa Carbaia, Artà
☎ 619 070 010
🕐 Apr–Oct Mon–Sat 10–1,
2.30–6.30; Nov–Mar Mon–
Sat 9–1, 2–5
💶 Inexpensive

HIGHLIGHT

● Shopping and sightseeing
in central Artà followed by a
night at the theatre (▷ 89).

TIP

● If you have a car, seek
out some of Mallorca's most
remote beaches north of
Artà: Cala Torta is signposted
via the road to Capdepera;
the pot-holed road discour-
ages many visitors so you
may have the place to
yourself.

**In the northeast of Mallorca, this ancient
town is overlooked by an impressive
castle and sanctuary while the streets
below are filled with arty boutiques. Artà
is the cultural capital of the area.**

Arty town Circling the hilltop Santuari de Sant
Salvador, Artà is a handsome, medium-sized town
with a lively cultural scene and a history of some
3,000 years. Begin on Artà's main thoroughfare,
Carrer del Ciutat, where the town's modern theatre is situated. The wide avenue narrows as you
head uphill past small shops and galleries. Arriving
at the steep-sided mound, your first stop will be at
the Esglesia Parroquial d'Artà (tel 971 836 020),
the parish church. Continue up the steps to the
Santuari de Sant Salvador, a fortified sanctuary
with a perimeter wall that you can walk around—
the views extend beyond Artà towards the north
coast's more remote beaches. The chapel dates
from 1825, replacing an earlier chapel, but the
walls were initially put up by Moors.

A history lesson However, even the sanctuary's
walls are pre-dated by Ses Països, a Talaiotic
village outside Artà, on the road to Capdepera.
Occupied by the Talaiots—Mallorca's pre-historic
people—from the 12th century BC, it still has an
impressive perimeter wall up to 3.5m (11ft) high
and a main gate with a lintel. If you don't make
it to Capocorb Vell (▷ 104), an hour here is a
good introduction to the Talaiots; there's more
information in the Museu Regional d'Artà on
Carrer Estel (tel 971 835 503; Tue–Fri 10–1).

From left: Cycling in Parc Natural de S'Albufera; S'Albufera wetlands

TOP 25

Parc Natural de S'Albufera

A staging post for migrating birds, the S'Albufera wetlands attract birders from across Europe in search of rare birds. Other visitors will find respite from the hectic beach resorts nearby.

Feathered friends Holidaymakers aren't the only creatures to arrive on Mallorca by air. Migrating birds use the island as a stopover and the marshes of this nature reserve are the best place to spot many unusual species. But even if you aren't an ardent birder, S'Albufera is a rewarding place to explore on foot or by bicycle, offering a soothing alternative to the beach resorts a short way along the bay.

Marshy maze S'Albufera's marshes have been recognized since Roman times for their birdlife, although the impetus in those days was to catch then consume the birds. But the area faced its greatest enemy in the form of a British company that began to drain the wetlands to harvest reeds and grow rice. Fortunately the scheme was stopped in time but not before the New Majorca Land Company had dug canals across S'Albufera. Many of the birding hides are now located along the park's canals, perfect for spotting reed warblers, water rails and the elusive moustached warbler. Predatory species include several varieties of heron and egret, osprey, falcons (peregrine and the rare Eleanora's) and owls. The park is criss-crossed by cycle paths, although most day-trippers stick to a circuit of the lagoon near the Sa Roca visitor centre.

THE BASICS

➕ H3
✉ Carretera Ma-12 Alcúdia–Can Picafort
☎ 971 892 250
🕐 Apr–Sep daily 9–6; Oct–Mar 9–5; visitor centre daily 9–4 all year
🍴 Restaurant at Grupotel Parc Natural (€–€€)
✋ Free, pass required from visitor centre

HIGHLIGHT

● If you don't know your reed warblers from your moustached warblers, pick up a leaflet identifying bird species from the visitor centre, settle down in a hide and wait. It's a curiously addictive activity.

TIP

● Picnics are not permitted in the reserve—but you can bring your own snacks and occupy a table at Sa Roca for a short while.

THE NORTHEAST TOP 25

More to See

CALA MILLOR

Cala Millor is a major holiday hotspot thanks to 2km (1 mile) of sandy beach. Summer sees the high-rise hotels filled with young sunseekers while an older generation takes over the resort in the low season.

✛ L5 🛈 Badia de Llevant, 2, tel 971 585 409

CALA RAJADA

Cala Rajada lies on the northeast corner of Mallorca. Once a fishing village, it is now an upmarket community dominated by expats. There are a lot of activities during the summer and nightlife is lively. Several beaches, other than the town's own Platja de Son Moll, are within reach. You can also take a ferry to Menorca from the port.

✛ M4 🛈 Plaça dels Pins, tel 971 563 033

CAN PICAFORT

Sprawled in the middle of the Badia d'Alcúdia, Can Picafort is the main north coast resort. Bars and souvenir shops proliferate behind the seafront promenade along the Passeig Colón. The principal appeal is the 13km (9-mile) beach although there are many activities such as go-karting and watersports.

✛ J3 🛈 Plaça Gabriel Roca, 6, tel 971 850 310

CAPDEPERA

Capdepera, on the road between Cala Rajada and Artà, is notable for one reason: its castle. With views of Menorca, Castell de Capdepera was built by King Jaume II in 1300 to guard against attacks from the sea but the site had been used by Romans and Moors.

✛ L4

Castell de Capdepera

✉ Carrer Castell ☎ 971 818 746 🕓 Apr–Oct daily 9–8; Nov–Mar 9–5 💶 Inexpensive ❓ Medieval market held third weekend of May

COVES D'ARTÀ

www.cuevasdearta.com

The east coast of Mallorca is riddled with caves and this complex of sea

Capdepera's castle overlooks the town

The caves near Artà are lit for the daily guided tours

caves at Cap Vermell errs on the side of entertainment rather than education. The caves were mapped by French geologist Édouard Martel in 1876, although they were previously occupied by pirates and even Moors hiding from Catalan forces. These days the caves have been embellished with sound-and-light shows and dramatic names such as Hell and Paradise. However, the natural wonder of the caves triumphs, with one cavern as large as Palma's cathedral and colossal stalactites hanging from the ceiling.

➕ M5 ✉ Carretera de las Cuevas, Capdepera ☎ 971 841 293 🕐 May–Oct daily 10–6; Nov–Apr 10–5 💵 Expensive

MUSEU ETNOLÒGIC DE MALLORCA

Muro, a working town on Mallorca's fertile central plain, is host to the Ethnological section of Palma's Museu de Mallorca. Housed in an imposing 17th-century palace, the museum's exhibits include rural tools and crafts. The collection of *siurells*, the small painted figures special to Mallorca, dates from 1955.

➕ H4 ✉ Carrer Major, 15, Muro ☎ 971 860 647 🕐 Tue–Sat 10–3, Sun 10–2 💵 Inexpensive

PUIG DE MARIA

The top of 'Mary's Mountain', on the outskirts of Pollença, is a spiritual place. There has been a church here since 1348 and a convent since 1371 and both remain up here. You can get a taste of the life the nuns live by staying overnight at the hostel.

➕ H2 ☎ 971 184 132 🚌 L340 to Pollença, then walk up the hill 💵 Free

PUNTA DE N'AMER

Punta de n'Amer is a wild and wooded nature reserve on the headland overlooking Cala Millor. It illustrates what the land must have looked like before the arrival of mass tourism. You can walk to the 200ha (495-acre) reserve from Cala Millor.

➕ L5 💵 Free

It's a lovely walk through citrus groves from Pollença to Puig de Maria

A watchtower in the Punta de n'Amer reserve

Shopping

BINIFELA

www.binifela.com

Organic produce, including herbs, honey, fruit and vegetables, is produced on this 15ha (37-acre) *finca* (estate), just to the north of Cala Rajada and Capdepera. Both English and German are spoken.

➕ L4 ✉ Carretera Cala Mesquida–Camí de Cala Moltó, Capdepera ☎ 971 819 034 🕐 Tue–Sat 9–2, other days by appointment

BODEGAS GALMÉS I RIBOT

www.galmesiribot.com

This family-run winery produces several wines from its 14ha (35-acre) vineyard with a variety of grapes including *prensal blanc* and *callet* from the Balearics and familiar varieties of chardonnay and merlot.

➕ H4 ✉ Son Llebre, Poligoni 8, Parc 41, Santa Margalida ☎ 687 789 932 🕐 Mon–Fri 9–1.30, 3–7; weekend tours by appointment

DOMUS ART

www.domusart.es

Imaginative interior decoration for dining rooms, living rooms and bedrooms.

➕ L4 ✉ Carrer Ciutat, 12, Artà ☎ 971 836 969 🕐 Daily 10–1, 5–8

ESPARTERIA JOSEP BERNAT

This small welcoming shop in Artà specializes in handmade espadrilles, straw hats, colourful wicker baskets, scarves and other accessories.

➕ L4 ✉ Carrer Anton Blanes, 21, Artà ☎ 971 836 389 🕐 Mon–Sat 10–1, 5–8, Sun 10–1

FORN DE CAN SEGURA

Buy fresh, handmade *ensaimadas* from this small shop in Muro.

➕ H4 ✉ Carrer Major 44, Muro ☎ 971 537 081 🕐 Daily 8–1

INTERSPORT

www.intersport.com

This sports shop is a one-stop solution if you are looking for sports clothes or equipment, be it tennis or jogging shoes, a football, T-shirts or even just a pair of sports socks.

➕ L4 ✉ Carrer Santa Margalida, 7, Artà ☎ 971 723 442 🕐 Mon–Sat 10–8

JOYERÍA KATIA

www.joyeriakatia.com

A wide selection of jewellery, ranging from diamond rings to pearl necklaces, is produced by this workshop in Cala Rajada (watches are also sold). There are branches throughout the northeast of the island, including Artà and Cala Millor.

➕ M4 ✉ Carrer Leonor Servera, 54, Cala Rajada ☎ 971 563 847 🕐 Mon–Sat 9.30–10.30, Sun 7–10

PEPNOT GALERIA

www.pepnotgaleria.com

Pepnot gallery displays the work of young, mostly Spanish, artists. Work is contemporary and includes paintings and sculpture.

➕ L4 ✉ Carrer Pep Not, 34, Artà ☎ 971 835 909 🕐 Tue, Wed, Fri 11–1, 5–8, Sat 11–1

SENYORA ANA

www.senyoraana.blogspot.com

The best place in Artà to buy traditionally made *sobrassada* (spicy Mallorcan sausages). Other deli items are also available.

➕ L4 ✉ Carrer Pere Amoros Esteva 9, Artà ☎ 971 835 911 🕐 Mon–Sat 10–1, 5–7

MARKETS

For a few hours a week, Mallorca's markets *(mercats)* transform towns into open-air bazaars where souvenirs, speciality foods and myriad other goods are traded. A selection of local markets:

Monday: Caimari, Manacor, Montuiri

Tuesday: Alcúdia, Artà, Campanet, Porreres

Wednesday: Andratx, Capdepera, Llucmajor, Petra, Port de Pollença, Santanyí, Sencelles, Sineu

Thursday: S'Arenal, San Llorenç, Inca

Friday: Algaida, Binissalem, Can Picafort, Llucmajor

Saturday: Bunyola, Cala Rajada, Sóller

Sunday: Alcúdia, Felanitx, Muro, Pollença, Porto Cristo, Valldemossa

---

Entertainment and Activities

AUDITORI D'ALCÚDIA

www.auditorialcudia.net

Alcúdia's bold auditorium is a modern venue for everything from ballet to jazz performances.

➕ J2 ✉ Plaça de la Porta de Mallorca, 3, Alcúdia ☎ 971 897 185

AUDITÒRIUM SA MÀNIGA

www.samaniga.es

Sa Màniga auditorium in Cala Millor has a 466-seat theatre staging drama, music and comedy.

➕ L5 ✉ Carrer de Son Galta, 4, Cala Millor ☎ 971 587 373

CANYAMEL GOLF CLUB

www.canyamelgolf.com

Rich in natural features, this is an 18-hole par-73 course in the northeast corner of the island.

➕ L4 ✉ Urbanización Canyamel, Avinguda d'Es Cap Vermell, Capdepera ☎ 971 841 313

HIDROPARK

www.hidroparkalcudia.com

Attractions at this water-park range from a heart-stopping 15m (49ft) slide to a reassuringly gentle wave pool. There is a separate area for smaller tots, plus go-karts and a mini-golf course. Food and drink must be purchased on site.

➕ J2 ✉ Avinguda Tucán, Port d'Alcúdia ☎ 971 891 672 ⏰ May–Oct daily 10–6. Closed Sun in May and Oct 💶 Expensive

KARTING CAN PICAFORT

www.kartingcanpicafort.com

This great go-kart track is the largest in Mallorca. The F1-themed café is next to a museum of vintage motorbikes. It's just outside Can Picafort on the road to Artà—a free bus runs from Can Picafort. All ages accepted.

➕ J3 ✉ Carretera Alcúdia–Artà ☎ 971 850 748 ⏰ May–Oct daily 10–10; Nov–Apr Tue–Sun 10–8 💶 Expensive

LUNA'S GRILL

www.lunasgrill.com

This Port d'Alcúdia cocktail bar and restaurant has live music nightly, as well as a children's play area. It gets packed at weekends, so arrive early to snag a table.

➕ J2 ✉ Avinguda de Pepe Mas, Port d'Alcúdia ☎ 971 892 333 ⏰ Daily 9am–late

---

WATERSPORTS

If you're tempted to try a new watersport, you will be spoiled for choice on Mallorca's north coast: tuition in waterskiing, jet-skiing, sailing, windsurfing and even kitesurfing is available from a number of operators. Before booking, check that instructors are qualified: dive centres should be PADI certified while some sailing centres are RYA or VDS (the German equivalent) approved.

PULA GOLF

www.pulagolf.com

Pula Golf was designed in part by Spanish player José Maria Olazabel. It's one of Mallorca's longest and most testing courses. Tuition is available from PGA professionals.

➕ L5 ✉ Carretera Son Cervera–Capdepera, km3, Son Cervera ☎ 971 817 034

SALAFÒNICA

www.myspace.com/salafonica

A long way, muscially and geographically, from the nightclubs in Mallorca's resorts, Salafònica is the island's home of underground dance music, attracting some of the hippest DJs in the world to this small inland town.

➕ H4 ✉ Carrer Germanies, Muro ☎ See website for details and flyers

TEATRE ARTÀ

www.teatrearta.com

Artà's handsome contemporary theatre is a thriving venue for drama, dance and music in this culturally minded community. It hosts a classical music festival in the summer.

➕ L4 ✉ Carrer de Ciutat, Artà ☎ 971 829 700

WINDFRIENDS

www.windfriends.com

Learn to sail, kitesurf or windsurf at this outfit in Alcúdia. A variety of courses is offered, from a few hours to several days.

➕ J2 ✉ Apartado de Correos, 178, Alcúdia ☎ 971 549 835 ⏰ May–Oct

Restaurants

PRICES

Prices are approximate, based on a 3-course meal for one person.

€€€	over €40
€€	€20–€40
€	under €20

CAFÉ PARISIEN (€–€€)

Café Parisien is the hub of Artà's social life. With WiFi and magazines, it's a popular place to catch up with the latest exhibitions over an espresso, while the food is whatever the market had available.

🚩 L4 ✉ Carrer de Ciutat, 18, Artà ☎ 971 835 440 🕐 Mon–Sat lunch and dinner

CASAL SANTA EULALIA (€€–€€€)

www.casal-santaeulalia.com
Chef Marcos Blanco updates Mallorcan cuisine in the wine cellar of this luxurious 13th-century manor house hotel on the road from Can Picafort to Santa Margalida. There's also a tapas bar and weekly barbecues in summer.

🚩 J4 ✉ Carretera Santa Margalida–Alcúdia, km1.8 ☎ 971 852 732 🕐 Daily dinner only 🛏 24 rooms

DHARMA CAFÉ (€)

Opened in 2014, this chilled-out café and restaurant in Alcúdia caters to vegetarian and vegan customers with an inventive menu that includes tasty salads and wonder-

ful soups (try the ice-cold avocado soup), and main dishes that change according to what is fresh in season. The desserts are superb and there is regular live music.

🚩 J2 ✉ Passeig Mare de Deu de la Victoria, 9, Alcúdia ☎ 971 577 750 🕐 Daily 9am–11.30pm

JARDÍN (€€€)

www.restaurantejardin.com
This Michelin-starred restaurant in Port d'Alcúdia is justifiably popular and has an inventive menu with dishes like lobster soup, oxtail with fungi ravioli, and strawberries with basil and tomatoes. The owners run the nearby (and similarly excellent) Bistro del Jardín.

🚩 J2 ✉ Tritones, Port d'Alcúdia ☎ 971 892 391 🕐 Tue–Sun lunch and dinner

MENU READER

What can you expect to see on Mallorcan menus? (▷ 106 for part two.)
Pa amb oli: crusty bread with garlic and tomatoes, sprinkled with sea salt and served with a bowl of olive oil.
Frit: a peasant dish. Chopped offal (lamb or pork) flavoured with wild fennel and mint then fried with potatoes and vegetables in oil.
Lomo con col: pork wrapped in cabbage leaves.
Tumbet: a Mallorcan ratatouille.

LA LOCANDA PARAISO DA MASSIMO (€–€€)

This restaurant brings Italian specialties, including *carpaccio* and *ossobucco*, to Cala Rajada, a town with a strong German presence. Risottos and fresh pasta—made in-house—are done well and the wine list has many Italian wines.

🚩 M4 ✉ Carrer Arquitecto Alomar, 20, Cala Rajada ☎ 971 563 045 🕐 Thu–Tue lunch and dinner. Closed late Nov–late Dec

MANTONIA (€€)

This Port d'Alcúdia restaurant has a bright contemporary interior and a predominantly Italian menu that also includes steaks and seafood. The setting is superb, overlooking the harbour. Reservations are advised at weekends.

🚩 J2 ✉ Carrer Teodoro Canet 2, Port d'Alcúdia ☎ 971 893 309 🕐 Wed–Mon lunch and dinner

SA PLAÇA (€€)

The best of the restaurant-cafés crowding Alcúdia's main square, Sa Plaça serves modern Mallorcan and Mediterranean cuisine in a spacious dining room. Spanish specialties include *piquillos* stuffed with salt cod. A children's menu is available.

🚩 J2 ✉ Plaça Constitució, 1, Alcúdia ☎ 971 546 278 🕐 Daily lunch and dinner. Closed Wed in winter

Beaches large and small, boat trips and *bodegas*: whether you love sunbathing, wine or just watching the waves, the southeast corner of Mallorca has plenty to offer visitors. The landscape is flat but not featureless; look out for hilltop hermitages and secret coves.

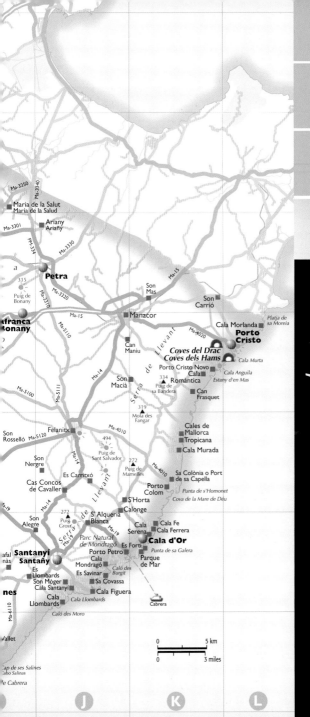

Ma-3250
Ma-3340

Maria de la Salut
Maria de la Salud

Ma-3301
Ariany
Ariañy

Ma-3330

PM-334
Petra

315
Puig de
Bonany

Ma-3310

Ma-3320

Son
Mas

Ma-15

Son
Carrió

Platja de
sa Moreia

afranca
onany

Ma-15

Manacor

Ma-4020

Cala Morlanda
Porto
Cristo

Ma-5110

Can
Maniu

*Coves del Drac
Coves dels Hams*

Cala Murta

Ma-5100

Son
Macià

Porto Cristo Novo
Cala
Romàntica

Cala Anguila
Estany d'en Mas

Ma-14

Ma-5111

314
Puig de
sa Bandera

Can
Frasquet

Son
Rosselló

Ma-5120

Felanitx

Ma-4010

319
Mola des
Fangar

Cales de
Mallorca
Tropicana
Cala Murada

494
Puig de
Sant Salvador

272
Puig de
Mamelles

Ma-4010

Sa Colònia o Port
de sa Capella

Son
Nergre

Ma-14

Es Carritxó

Porto
Colom

Punta de s'Homonet
Cova de la Mare de Déu

Cas Concos
de Cavaller

Serra de Llevant

S'Horta

A-19

Ma-14

272
Puig
Gross

Calonge

Son
Alegre

Serra de Llevant

Ma-19

S' Alqueria
Blanca

Cala
Serena

Cala Fe
Cala Ferrera

afal
nàs

Santanyi
Santañy

*Parc Natural
de Mondragó*

Es Forti
Cala d'Or

Punta de sa Galera

nes

Es
Llombards
Son Möger
Cala Santanyi

Porto Petro
Cala
Mondragó
Es Savinar

Parque
de Mar

Ma-6110

Cala
Llombards

Sa Covassa

Caló des
Burgit

Cala Figuera

Cabrera

Cala Llombards

allet

Caló des Moro

0   5 km

0   3 miles

Cap de ses Salines
Cabo Salinas

e Cabrera

J   K   L

Cala d'Or and Beaches

TOP 25

From left: The beach at Cala d'Or; relaxing at Cala d'Or's marina; a typical rocky cove

THE BASICS

⊞ K8
ℹ Avinguda Perico Pomar, 10, Cala d'Or, tel 971 657 463
🚌 From Palma via Santanyí

Cala Mondragó
⊞ G2
✉ Carretera Ma-19 (parking at Ses Fonts de n'Alis)
☎ 971 181 022
🕐 Information point: daily 9–4
♿ Access to Cala Mondragó

HIGHLIGHT

● Explore the rocky headlands and sandy coves of Parc Natural Cala Mondragó while keeping an eye out for the area's wildlife.

TIP

● The tourist office can advise which beaches are the most suitable for young children and for people with mobility problems.

The beaches of Cala d'Or provide perhaps the best balance between accessibility and attractiveness on the island. These rocky coves have survived the onslaught of tourism and there is a nature reserve at Cala Mondragó.

Beach life For many visitors to Mallorca, the beach is an indispensable part of the holiday. The east coast has many of the most popular beaches, not least the Cales de Mallorca, lying between Porto Cristo and Porto Colom, adjacent to Manacor. S'Illot is a medium-sized resort with lots of activities based on the broad beach, while Cala Anguila and Cala Mendia are quieter, more residential areas.

Sandy coves Further south lie the coves of Cala d'Or. This stretch of coast, south of Porto Colom and accessed via Santanyí, has a great variety of beaches from tiny Cala Brafi to the 100m (300ft) of Cala d'Or itself. There are beaches in urban areas and those, like Cala Mondragó, where you can imagine that you're marooned on a deserted island. Cala d'Or takes its name from the chic local port where yachts have long since replaced the fishing boats. Strolling around the harbour and its whitewashed properties is a pleasant way to spend an evening after a day at the beach, or head for Porto Colom's restaurants. Another good spot for fish restaurants is Cala Figuera, a pretty fishing village south of Cala Mondragó. But for a truly unspoiled beach experience, Cala Mondragó should be your destination.

Coves del Drac and Coves dels Hams

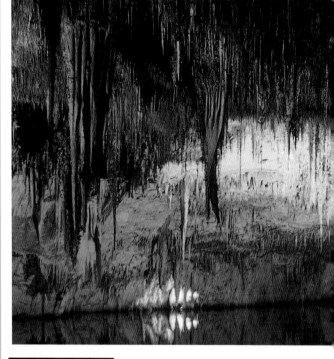

HIGHLIGHT

● The love-it-or-hate-it lighting by Buigas includes a subterranean sunrise over Lake Martel.

TIPS

● Surfaces can be wet and slippery; wear suitable shoes.
● Avoid the tour groups by arriving for the last tour of the day.

These two cave systems are Mallorca's most spectacular. With vast caverns named the Enchanted City and the Fairies' Theatre, expect to be transported to a dramatically lit watery underworld. They are a popular day trip.

In the dark The caves of the Dragon are one of Mallorca's top sights but don't turn up expecting a naturalistic experience. The cave network was developed by French speleologist Édouard Martel in 1896 and in the intervening years they have become a spectacular destination, with elaborate illuminations and classical concerts.

Rock stars None of this detracts too much from the stunning scale and beauty of the rock formations and caverns, which have been given

Clockwise from left: Reflections in the waterpools at the Coves del Drac enhance the lighting effects; a section of the Coves del Drac known as Baños de Diana (Diana's Baths); the entrance to the Coves del Drac; a limestone shawl shows variations in mineral composition

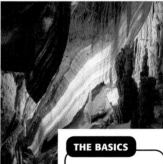

evocative names such as the Fairies' Theatre and the Enchanted City. Diana's Bath is one of the most awe-inspiring spots, with thousands of delicate white stalactites hanging from the cave ceiling over a glassy pool.

Light fantastic None of this was enough for engineer Carles Buigas (1898–1979), who spent years rigging electric lighting throughout the caves, eventually requiring 100,000 watts to power it all. The culmination of the tour, which takes an hour, is your arrival at Lake Martel. The underground lake is the setting for a classical concert conducted from two illuminated rowing boats. The Coves del Drac is a crowd-pleasing extravaganza but for a less busy day choose the Coves dels Hams near Porto Cristo. They too are illuminated and have a concert.

THE BASICS

➕ K6–L6

Coves del Drac
www.cuevasdeldrach.com
✉ Carretera de las Cuevas, Porto Cristo
☎ 971 820 753
🕐 Apr/Mar–Oct daily tours at 10, 11, 12, 2, 3, 4, 5; Nov–Mar daily tours at 10.45, 12, 2, 3.30, 4.30 (no concert)
💰 Expensive
🍴 Bar and café (€)

Coves dels Hams
www.cuevas-hams.com
✉ Carretera Ma-4020 Manacor–Porto Cristo
☎ 971 820 988
🕐 Jun–Sep daily 10–5; Oct–May 11–5
💰 Expensive

Illa de Cabrera and Other Boat Trips

From left: Explore Illa de Cabrera on foot—or take an excursion around the island

Join boat trips to visit a one-time prison island named after its resident goats, an island named after the dragon it resembles and even Mallorca's sister Balearic island of Menorca.

Water world There are few things more refreshing and relaxing than a boat trip and Mallorca has several popular routes to consider. Two tiny islands lie just offshore: Sa Dragonera (▷ 48–49) and Illa de Cabrera, 10km (6 miles) by boat from the southeast town of Colònia de Sant Jordi. Cabrera—'Goat Island'—has a dark history but its present incarnation is far less mysterious: it's a national park and home to several endangered species including the Balearic lizard, Balearic shearwaters and Andouin's gull. Birds of prey include ospreys, peregrines and Eleanora's falcon.

Prison island Due to the sensitive habitats on Cabrera, visitors follow a guided tour of the island which takes in the 14th-century castle above the harbour and a basic museum in Can Feliu, an old wine cellar. However, conditions today are far less restrictive than they were for the castle's inhabitants during the Napoleonic Wars. These French prisoners were starved of regular supplies and had to introduce rats and lizards to their diet.

Sightseeing by sea Other boat trips depart from several ports; many journeys go via the Bay of Palma. More ambitious mariners can take a ferry all the way from Port d'Alcúdia to Menorca, or from Palma to Ibiza or mainland Spain.

Petra

From left: Petra's main square; a portrait of Junípero Serra; Serra's father's house

Petra is a deceptively sleepy town: it played a key role in Mallorca's history as the birthplace of its most famous son, Father Junípero Serra. See his home and a museum plus nearby Ermita de Bonany.

On a mission In the heart of Mallorca, between Manacor and Sineu, Petra is a quietly modest town but for one claim to fame: Father Junípero Serra was born here in 1713. The young priest had wider horizons and, after being ordained in Palma in 1749, he departed Mallorca for Mexico. Twenty years after he arrived in Mexico he had made his way to the Californian coast where he began to found missions; these missions, among them San Diego and San Francisco, would grow into some of America's greatest cities.

Father's house The house of Junípero Serra's parents is open to the public but you will have to ask the caretaker to open it up for you. Also in town is the San Bernardino convent where Serra was educated. The streets around the family house are decorated with *majolica* tiles depicting his exploits in Mexico and America.

Serra's sermon Just south of Petra, at the end of a narrow lane, lies the Ermita de Bonany, the hermitage where Serra delivered his last sermon before leaving Mallorca. The hermitage stands on a hilltop with superb views of the surrounding countryside; like many of the hermitages around Mallorca you can stay overnight in a basic cell here, although the nearest source of food is Petra.

THE BASICS

✚ J5

Casa Museu Fra Junípero Serra
✉ Carrer Barracar Alt, 6, Petra
☎ 971 561 028, 971 561 149
🕐 By appointment with the caretaker at Carrer Barracar Baix, 2
💷 Donation requested
🍴 Es Cellar (€€) restaurant, ▷ 106

HIGHLIGHT

● Watching the sun go down from the terrace of Ermita de Bonany.

TIP

● Time your visit to Petra with the Wednesday market in nearby Sineu and pick up some fresh produce. Or stop in Vilafranca de Bonany, famed for its fruit and vegetables.

INLAND, EAST AND THE SOUTH TOP 25

Wine Tasting

Take time to look around one of the island's family-run bodegas

THE BASICS

Jaume Mesquida
www.jaumemesquida.com
🗓 H6
✉ Carrer Vileta, 7, Porreres
☎ 971 647 106
🕐 Mon–Fri 8–7, Sat 10–2
♿ Wine labels in Braille, access good for wheelchairs

Miquel Oliver
www.miqueloliver.com
🗓 J5
✉ Carrer Font, 26, Petra
☎ 971 561 117
🕐 Mon–Fri 10–1.45, 3.30–6 (Jul, Aug 10–3)

Bodegues Macià Batle
www.maciabatle.com
🗓 F5
✉ Camí de Coanegra, Santa Maria del Camí
☎ 971 140 014
🕐 Mid-Jun to mid-Oct Mon–Fri 9–7; mid-Oct to mid-Jun Mon–Fri 9–6.30, Sat 9.30–1

Discover the little-known world of Mallorcan wine. Produced by friendly, family-run *bodegas* from indigenous grapes, Mallorcan wine is the next big thing on the island.

Wine time 'This is a good time for Mallorcan wine.' So says Bàrbara Mesquida Mora, the managing director of Jaume Mesquida and the fourth generation of her family to run the *bodega*. Mallorcan wine is becoming more widely respected, although only tiny quantities are exported. Jaume Mesquida is one of many small, family-run vineyards across the main wine-producing area of Mallorca, including the two Protected Designations of Origin (PDO) on the island: Binissalem and Vi des Pla I Llevant. Most of the vineyards are on the flat plains around the towns of Binissalem and Felanitx and many of them welcome visitors with wine tastings and tours of the cellars.

Brilliant *bodegas* Three of the best *bodegas*, for the tours and the wine, are: Jaume Mesquida in Porreres (near Felanitx), Miquel Oliver in Petra and Macià Batle, a large winery near Binissalem. Miquel Oliver is run by Miquel Oliver, his daughter Pilar and her husband Jaume. Macia Batle, one of the oldest wineries on Mallorca, is based on an estate founded in 1856 and specializes in the indigenous grapes of Callet and Manto Negra. You can take an organized tour of select *bodegas* with www.majorcawinetour.com and allow someone else to do the driving.

More to See

COLÒNIA DE SANT JORDI

This is one of the key towns on the south coast: boat trips to Illa de Cabrera (▷ 98) depart from the port and there are several beaches, including Mallorca's famous nudist beach, Es Trenc, to the west, within a short drive. Colònia de Sant Jordi itself has a central beach and promenade (Platja d'es Port). The Parque Nacional del Archipiélago de Cabrera is also headquartered in the town and the Cabrera Interpretation Centre (Carrer Gabriel Roca, tel 971 656 282; daily 10–2.30, 3–6; summer till 8) explains the biodiversity of the area and the conservation programme.

➕ G8 ℹ️ Carrer Doctor Barraquer, 5, tel 971 656 073

COVES DE CAMPANET

www.covesdecampanet.com

Nestled in the northwest corner of this region, in the shadow of the Serra de Tramuntana, this is Mallorca's smallest cave system that is open to the public but it is no less fascinating than the bigger attractions. A tour of the limestone caverns takes about 40 minutes and your guide will point out not only the strange limestone formations but also fossils.

➕ G3 ✉️ Camí de ses Coves, Campanet ☎ 971 516 130 🕐 Apr–Sep daily 10–7; Oct–Mar 10–6 (last tour 1 hour before closing) 💰 Expensive

INCA

One of Mallorca's main commercial hubs, Inca is noted for its leather products, although the city's factory outlets are suffering from the close proximity of the Festival Park retail complex (▷ 105) and bargains are sometimes thin on the ground. The lively weekly market, the island's largest, takes place in Plaça d'Espanya on Thursdays and is a better option for souvenir hunting.

➕ G4 🚉 From Palma ❓ Market Thu

PORTO CRISTO

With pleasant beaches and a relaxed air, Porto Cristo is a quieter option

The entrance to the Coves de Campanet

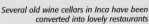

Several old wine cellars in Inca have been converted into lovely restaurants

than the more developed resorts along the east coast although there are several hotels and restaurants along the beachfront with views across the water. It is also well placed for many of the area's main attractions, including the Coves del Drac (▷ 96–97), a series of vast underground caverns, just to the southwest of town.

➕ L6 🛈 Carrer Moll, tel 971 815 103

PUIG DE RANDA AND SANTUARI DE CURA

www.santuaridecura.org

Look left on the road from Algaida to Llucmajor and you'll spot the Puig de Randa, a conical hill with the Santuari de Cura perched right on top. The Santuari was Mallorca's first hermitage and was founded by Ramón Llull in 1275; however, the present monastery dates from the 17th and 20th centuries. There are superb views all the way to the Serra de Tramuntana from the monastery's viewpoint. Two more hermitages stand on the hillside above Randa, a

small village with an excellent hotel and restaurant (▷ 106, 111).

➕ G6

Santuari de Nostra Senyora de Cura

☎ 971 660 994 🕐 Daily 10.30–1.30, 2.30–6.30 💰 Donation requested

SANTA EUGÈNIA

Surrounded by typically Mallorcan almond orchards, Santa Eugènia represents the rural Mallorca of Es Pla, the flat, fertile plain stretching across the southeast of the island. Natura Park on the outskirts of the village is a wildlife park popular with families. Some enjoyably easy walking routes circle the village.

➕ F5 🍴 Bars and cafés nearby

SANTA MARÍA DEL CAMÍ

The market town of Santa María is set where the mountains meet the plain and is the gateway to some great walking country. It's not far from Palma and there are several attractions in the vicinity, including Festival Park (▷ 105) and a proliferation of *bodegas*. However, the main

The village of Randa is at the foot of the Puig de Randa

A cove near Santanyí

motorway from Palma to Pollença puts off many visitors from staying long, unless you have a reservation at the exclusive Read's Hotel (▷ 112).
➕ F5 🚌 From Palma 🍴 Read's Hotel (€€€)

SANTANYÍ

Many of the southeast's best beaches are reached via Santanyí—but don't rush through; this gorgeously golden town merits a little more time. The honeyed sandstone used in Palma's cathedral comes from Santanyí and the town looks wonderful in the light of a setting sun.
➕ J8 🍴 Local cafés, bars and restaurants
❓ Wed and Sat are market days

SES SALINES

Much of Mallorca's salt comes from this town's salt pans, which attract migrant bird species and flocks of birders. If you're not interested in birds, how about cacti? The botanical garden Botanicactus has one of the world's largest cactus collections with more than 400 varieties.
➕ H8

Botanicactus

www.botanicactus.com
➕ H8 ✉ Carretera Ma-6100 Ses Salines–Santanyí ☎ 971 649 494 🕐 May–Aug daily 9–7; Sep, Oct, Feb–Apr 9–5.30; Nov–Jan 10.30–4.30 ✋ Moderate

VILAFRANCA DE BONANY

This rural town produces many of Mallorca's vegetables and the evidence hangs from shopfronts across the town. Apart from the hanging bunches of tomatoes, peppers and garlic, Vilafranca's other important product is the honeydew melon. The rural life and traditions of the area are explored at the Els Calderers manor house. Here you can see the estate's wine cellar, granary, bakery and chapel before sampling some delicious home-made products.
➕ H6 ❓ Melon festival in Sep

Els Calderers

➕ H6 ✉ Carretera Ma-3222 Sant Joan–Vilafranca de Bonany ☎ 971 526 069
🕐 Apr–Oct daily 10–6; Nov–Mar 10–5
✋ Moderate

Just some of the cacti on display at Botanicactus near Ses Salines

A colourful fruit and vegetable stall at Vilafranca de Bonany

Almonds and Ancient Ruins

Quiet lanes through almond orchards and flat countryside make this bike ride suitable for all, but bring some water and take it easy.

DISTANCE: 25km (15.5 miles) **ALLOW:** 3 hours plus stops

START **END**

THE POLICE STATION ON CAMÍ DE S'AGUILA, LLUCMAJOR
✚ G6 🚍 Palma–Llucmajor L501, L502

THE POLICE STATION ON CAMÍ DE S'AGUILA, LLUCMAJOR

❶ Follow the Camí de S'Aguila south, away from Llucmajor. Cross over the new motorway and carry straight on, following the Camí de Cas Busso. At the mini-crossroad go straight over, signed Talaiot.

❼ Just before you meet the motor-way you turn right then left to get back onto the flyover to cross the motor-way. Head back into Llucmajor.

❻ After about 11km (7 miles), follow the road round to the right then take the left fork, signposted Llucmajor and Camí de S'Aguila.

❷ This straight, wide and little-used road has tumbled-down dry-stone walls on either side and beyond them, fields of almond trees. If you ride the route in spring, there may be wild flowers carpeting the fields. Continue on this road.

❺ Follow the Camí de Betlem. At the stop sign, go straight ahead, signposted Llucmajor and Camí de S'Aguila. After the sharp right corner, the lane narrows and becomes more overgrown.

❸ The road bends to the left before the next junction, where there's a café, Cas Busson, on the left. Go right at the junction with the main road, sign-posted Talaiot, S'Arenal and Cala Pi.

❹ Ride for 1km (0.6 mile) along the main road before reaching the ancient site of Capocorb Vell, on the right. Just after the roadside car park, take the right turn signposted Camí de Betlem.

Shopping

CAN MAJORAL
www.canmajoral.com
Family of winemakers growing organic grapes—both indigenous and foreign—for a range of reds and whites.
🞖 G6 ✉ Carrer del Campanar, Algaida ☎ 971 665 867 🕓 Mon–Fri 4–8, Sat 9–1

FESTIVAL PARK
www.festivalpark.es
The factory shops of Inca have taken a blow from the Festival Park shopping complex, where there are shops from small boutiques to global brands and factory outlets. Clothes and shoe shops figure prominently, including a branch of Mallorca's own walking boots company, Bestard. There are fast food outlets and cafés, cinemas

> **PAYMENT**
>
> Most larger shops accept credit cards but euros will be preferred in smaller shops and in shops in the villages. When buying from farms, markets and other local producers only euros will be accepted.

and a bowling alley.
🞖 F5 ✉ Carretera Palma–Inca, km7.1, Santa Maria del Camí exit ☎ 971 140 925 🕓 Daily 10–10 (Sun 10–9)

FORMATGES BURGUERA
www.formatgesburguera.com
This family business makes traditional Mallorcan cheese from local cow's milk, including a semi-smoked cheese.
🞖 H7 ✉ Carretera Campos–Colònia Sant Jordí, km7, Campos ☎ 971 655 435 🕓 Mon–Fri 8–11, 3–7, Sat, Sun 3.30–6.30

Entertainment and Activities

CLUB NÀUTIC PORTOCOLOM
www.cnportocolom.com
Portocolom's marina and yacht club offers sailing lessons and fishing trips.
🞖 K7 ✉ Carrer Pescadors, 23, Portocolom ☎ 971 824 658

CLUB VOL ILIURE
www.clubdevolmediterrani.com
This Petra-based venture offers hang-gliding courses catering to a wide range of abilities, from one-off sessions for experienced hang-gliders to intensive weekend sessions for beginners.
🞖 J5 ✉ Carrer Bellavista, Petra ☎ 655 766 443

GOLF SON ANTEM I AND II
www.marriott.com
Marriott's gold resort at Son Antem has two 18-hole courses, a driving range and a golf academy.
🞖 G7 ✉ Carretera Ma-19, exit 20, Llucmajor ☎ 971 129 100

OBSERVATORIO ASTRONÓMICO MALLORCA
www.mallorcaplanetarium.com
Mallorca's observatory and planetarium stages shows and events for children (shows at 8pm) and is an interesting place to look around.
🞖 G5 ✉ Camí de l'Observatori, Costitx ☎ 971 513 344 (from 9.30–1.30) 🕓 Tue–Sat

SON MENUT
www.sonmenut.com
This *finca* close to Felanitx offers riding lessons and guided excursions on horseback, lasting from an hour to a whole day's ride at Es Trenc beach. Suitable for all ages and levels of experience.
🞖 J7 ✉ Carretera Felanitx–Campos, km7.5 ☎ 971 582 920

Restaurants

PRICES

Prices are approximate, based on a 3-course meal for one person.

€€€	over €40
€€	€20–€40
€	under €20

ES 4 VENTS (€€)

One of a trio of excellent roadside restaurants at the junction of the old Palma–Manacor road (now bypassed by a motorway). Es 4 Vents attracts a loyal crowd at weekends with its hearty but sophisticated Mallorcan dishes. Alternatives nearby are Ca'n Mateu and Cal Dimoni, which flame-grills meat and sausages.

🔹 G6 ✉ Carretera Palma–Manacor, km21.7, Algaida ☎ 971 665 173 ⏰ Fri–Wed lunch and dinner

CAN A BEL (€€)

This place has a cool urban chic atmosphere and a great menu of hearty local tapas and main dishes. It is a great place to start the day, reputedly serving the best coffee in town—enjoy a cup with a traditional Catalan breakfast of *tostada* (toast) topped with crushed tomatoes, olive oil and garlic. There is live music occasionally in the evenings.

🔹 J5 ✉ Plaça Ramón Llull, 5, Petra ☎ 971 561 599 ⏰ Mon–Sat breakfast, lunch and dinner, Sun breakfast and lunch

ES CELLER (€–€€)

Venture down the stone steps in Petra's best cellar restaurant and prepare for roasted pork or lamb from the log-fired oven in the dining room.

🔹 J5 ✉ Carrer de l'Hospital, 46, Petra ☎ 971 561 056 ⏰ Tue–Sun lunch and dinner

DOLC Y DOLC (€)

At this no-frills café and pizzeria tucked up a side street in Petra the pizzas are well-priced, piled high and superb. A perfect budget option.

🔹 J5 ✉ Carrer Sol, Petra ⏰ Tue–Sat lunch and dinner

MENU READER

Part two of what you can expect to see on a Mallorcan menu (▷ 90 for part one):

Cordero lechali: roast lamb. Typically served as a slow-roasted shoulder with rosemary and garlic.

Arroz brut: 'dirty' rice. Meat, vegetables and rice flavoured together with *sobrassada*, a moist, spicy sausage.

Caracoles: snails served with the rich, garlic mayonnaise *aioli*.

Ensaimada: a spiral-shaped pastry that contains either a sweet or savoury filling.

Bunyols: potato fritters dipped in sugar and served with apricot jam.

Gato de Almendra: a light, almondy sponge cake.

Herbes: the local aniseed-flavoured *digestif*.

ES LLAUT (€€€)

www.solmelia.com

A chic hotel restaurant, Es Llaut serves a well-balanced menu featuring local ingredients. Try rabbit with sun-dried tomato risotto or sea bream in an olive crust. Dessert might be accompanied by a cactus sorbet, which tastes better than it sounds.

🔹 K8 ✉ Meliá Cala d'Or Boutique Hotel, Carrer Portinatx, 16–18, Cala d'Or ☎ 971 648 181 ⏰ Daily dinner only

SA PLAÇA (€€)

At this small but pretty restaurant on the ground floor of the Sa Plaça hotel, the chef adds a modern twist to Mallorcan dishes. Lighter meals such as fish or salads are excellent. The *menú del día* is good value.

🔹 J5 ✉ Plaça Ramón Llull, 4, Petra ☎ 971 561 646 ⏰ Wed–Mon breakfast, lunch, dinner ❓ Three bedrooms

ES RECÓ DE RANDA (€€€)

www.esrecoderanda.com

The standout restaurant in this part of the interior, Es Recó de Randa has a lunchtime menu of light dishes and an à la carte menu in the evening. There's an attractive terrace looking out over the countryside, plus a bar. Cooking and service are of a high standard.

🔹 G6 ✉ Carrer Font, 21, Randa ☎ 971 660 997 ⏰ Daily lunch and dinner

Accommodation on Mallorca has improved greatly. Gone are the high-rise hotels along the seafronts. Instead, there is a huge variety of places to stay for every pocket and the standard is increasing all the time.

Introduction

Urban or rural, beachfront or mountain-top, palace or apartment: there's excellent accommodation across the island. Book in advance for the prime places.

What's Available

Even on this compact island, it pays to be selective about where you stay. In the heat of summer the narrow roads of the Tramuntana are often congested with coaches, so many of the hotels in the mountains are better in the shoulder months of May, June, September and October. Similarly, many of the beach resorts are deserted out of the high season and many hotels on the island close for the winter. During the summer months the resorts are typically the preserve of the package holiday companies and accommodation may be on a full-board basis—but often hotels will include breakfast in the basic price. Many hotels, especially the better independent hotels under the Reis de Mallorca banner, have excellent restaurants where the evening meals aren't to be missed.

Pricing

Most hotel prices are adjusted seasonally but a few hotels at the very top end keep rates constant all the year. Many hotels will double their prices according to demand during the summer school holidays—booking very early or very late may help. If booking direct during the quieter seasons, always check whether there are any deals available, such as four nights for the price of three. Rates are monitored by the local government and have to be posted up in the foyers of each hotel and also detail the IVA tax levied (currently 7 per cent).

RECENT DEVELOPMENTS

There's a bewildering choice of hotel types, from ultra-stylish boutique hotels to rustic estates (*fincas* and *agro-turismos*) that now welcome guests. As more independent travellers arrive in Mallorca, the typical resort hotel, mostly booked in advance by travel agents, is losing favour, to be replaced by smaller, snazzier beach clubs.

From top to bottom: Hotel Mar i Vent; Hotel Bon Sol; the garden of Hotel San Lorenzo; understated style in Alcúdia

Budget Hotels

PRICES

Expect to pay under €75 per night for a budget hotel room.

EL GUIA

www.sollernet.com/elguia
In a typical Mallorcan townhouse, this delightful hotel in Sóller maximizes the charm of its traditional surroundings. Rooms are furnished with dark wood furniture and pretty fabrics; several have views of the mountains. Breakfast features local produce. The friendly owner can advise on all aspects of sightseeing in town.
➕ E3 ✉ Carrer Castanyer, 2, Sóller ☎ 971 630 227

HOSPEDERÍA SANTUARI DE CURA

www.santuariodecura.com
The hostelry of the Sanctuary at the summit of the Puig de Randa isn't as basic as you'd expect from a Franciscan monastery. The 31 rooms have television, bathrooms and internet access. But it's still a peaceful, restful place. A restaurant serves traditional local food and there's a museum dedicated Ramón Llull.
➕ G6 ✉ Santuari de Cura, Puig de Randa, Randa ☎ 971 120 260

HOSTAL RITZI

www.hostalritzi.com
The Ritzi is an older hostal, so is a little scuffed in places. The rooms are comfortable enough, however, and a Continental breakfast is included in the price. Its chief appeal is its central location in Palma's tapas quarter, although this can mean that it gets noisy. Pack your earplugs!
➕ c3 ✉ Carrer Apuntadores, 6, Palma ☎ 971 714 610

HOSTAL SAN TELMO

www.hostalsantelmo.com
Situated just 200m (218 yds) from the beach, this Palma hotel is ideally placed. The comfortable rooms are furnished with light pine furniture. The cheaper options share a bathroom. Facilities include free WiFi, parking and a swimming pool.
➕ a3 (fold out map)
✉ Carrer Antoni Gelabert, 4, Cala Mayor, Palma ☎ 971 400 464

HOTEL BORN

www.hotelborn.com
Consistently popular, the Born is Palma's best budget hotel and needs

SELF-CATERING

Some hotels offer self-catering apartments or suites but the best-value self-catering accommodation is found by renting privately owned villas, townhouses and *casas rurales*. Most are advertised on the internet by their owners. Rates are variable during the year with July and August often the most expensive.

to be booked in advance. Rooms are set around a pretty courtyard in the 16th-century palace and have basic furnishings, including a bathroom and air conditioning. Service is friendly and helpful.
➕ c2 ✉ Carrer Sant Jaume, 3, Palma ☎ 971 712 942

HOTEL RURAL SON JORDÁ

www.sonjorda.com
There's little to do at Son Jordá other than laze by the pool or play a game of tennis; the converted *finca* is in the rural heartland of Mallorca with the closest towns being Sencelles and Sineu. The hotel has 20 rooms.
➕ G5 ✉ Carretera Sineu km24, Ruberts ☎ 971 872 279 ⏰ Closed Dec–Feb

S'HORTA

www.finca-shorta.com
With prices from €74 for a studio (outside the high season), this *agroturismo* represents good value for money for accommodation in this corner of the island. It is about 1km (0.6 miles) from the beach at Cala Aguila, and Artà's entertainment is equally accessible. Facilities include a swimming pool and barbecue. Children and pets are welcome. The farmhouse conveniently offers any length of stay from one night upwards.
➕ L4 ✉ Camí S'Horta, Capdepera ☎ 600 232 627 ⏰ Closed Dec–Feb

Mid-Range Hotels

AIMIA HOTEL
www.aimiahotel.com
Perhaps Port de Sóller's most stylish hotel, the Aimia's interior is sleek and functional; the 43 rooms are compact but uncluttered. There's a secluded pool area, a bar and restaurant plus weekly activities.
✚ E3 ✉ Carrer Santa María del Camí, 1, Port de Sóller ☎ 971 631 200 ◷ Closed mid-Nov to Feb

CA'N VERDERA
www.canverdera.com
Mallorca's prettiest village in the Tramuntana, Fornalutx is an ideal mountain hideaway, if you can stand the day-trippers. Fortunately, you're insulated from them in Ca'n Verdera, a small, chic hotel overlooking the valley. The 11 rooms are coolly comfortable and a tree-lined pool beckons.
✚ E3 ✉ Carrer Toros, 1, Fornalutx ☎ 971 638 203 ◷ Closed mid-Nov to Feb

HOTEL BON SOL
www.hotelbonsol.es
Martin Xamena's guests at the Bon Sol often return year after year. The hotel is traditional and has outstanding service from longstanding staff.

Highlights are a terrace restaurant on a tiny cove and a pool surrounded by tropical gardens.
✚ D6 ✉ Passeig d'Illetes, 30 ☎ 971 402 111 ◷ Closed late Nov to mid-Dec

HOTEL DALT MURADA
www.daltmurada.com
Dalt Murada's rooms haven't been updated in a while but the solid furnishings and antiques mean that doesn't matter. Bathrooms tend to be huge, with freestanding baths. Breakfast is basic but the quiet location close to the Palau d'Almudaina is very convenient.
✚ d3 ✉ Carrer Almudaina, 6a, Palma ☎ 971 425 300

HOTEL MAR I VENT
www.hotelmarivent.com
The views over the Mediterranean from the

Mar i Vent are unrivalled. The family-run hotel in Banyalbufar has a pool and a terrace where you can take breakfast. Décor in the 29 rooms is traditionally Mallorcan.
✚ C4 ✉ Carrer Major, 49, Banyalbufar ☎ 971 618 000

HOTEL MELIÁ CALA D'OR BOUTIQUE HOTEL
www.solmelia.com
This mini-complex of whitewashed buildings has a wide range of accommodation a short walk from Cala d'Or's beach. For just 49 rooms there are three restaurants, three pools, with shady areas, a state-of-the-art spa and a gym. The junior suites have their kitchens but try Es Llaut restaurant (▷ 106) at least once.
✚ K8 ✉ Carrer Portinatx 16–18, Cala d'Or ☎ 971 648 181 ◷ Closed Nov–Feb

HOTEL ES MOLÍ
www.esmoli.com
One of the largest hotels in the Tramuntana, with 87 rooms, Es Molí has a loyal group of largely English guests who come for the expert service and uncomplicated facilities. Both the décor and dining are traditional while the setting, surrounded by gardens in the lee of the mountains, is fantastic.
✚ D4 ✉ Carretera Valldemossa–Deià, Deià ☎ 971 639 000 ◷ Closed Nov–Mar

HOTEL NORD

www.hotelruralnord.com
This rustic and peaceful hotel has eight rooms; décor is simple (plain white bedlinen) but classic. Breakfast showcases several local products and dinner is cooked on request. Staff are very friendly and the village of Estellencs has escaped most of the development of the Tramuntana. Tip: don't try driving to the front door; park in the village and walk down to the hotel.

⊞ C5 ⊠ Plaça d'Es Triquet, 4, Estellencs ☎ 971 149 006
⊛ Closed Nov–Jan

HOTEL ES RECÓ DE RANDA

www.esrecoderanda.com
At the foot of the Puig de Randa, Es Recó is the best hotel in the area. Justifiably, it prides itself on the excellent kitchen; its regular paella night is recommended. The 14 rooms are varied in size and aspect but all are full of character and many have great views of the Tramuntana.

⊞ G6 ⊠ Carrer Font, 21, Randa ☎ 971 660 997

HOTEL SAN LORENZO

www.hotelsanlorenzo.com
San Lorenzo is small but delightful, with a great location in Palma's old town. The townhouse's nine rooms are individually decorated; the suites have their terraces and are much more private.

The pool is better suited to dips rather than laps.
⊞ b3 (fold-out map)
⊠ Carrer San Lorenzo, 14, Palma ☎ 971 728 200

HOTEL TRES

www.hoteltres.com
There's a lot to like at Palma's Hotel Tres, including its rooftop terrace with unbeatable views of the cathedral and the hip, glass-fronted bar area opening onto the courtyard. If you don't want to eat, drink or relax in the hotel, La Llotja is on the doorstep.
⊞ c3 ⊠ Carrer Apuntadors, 3, Palma ☎ 971 717 333

MONNABER NOU

www.monnaber.com
A restored 13th-century manor house in the foothills of the Tramuntana houses this family-friendly hotel, complete with a children's swimming pool. It abides by a strong eco-friendly ethos: solar panels provide energy for 80 per cent of the hotel's hot water. There are 25 rooms on this huge country estate; some rooms

WATER-WISE

Conservation of water is an issue on Mallorca and hotels will ask you to be selective about laundry and to turn off taps when brushing your teeth. Some hotels are starting to recycle their grey water, which deserves to be encouraged.

overlooking the interior courtyard can be dark.
⊞ G3 ⊠ Campanet
☎ 971 877 176

POLLENTIA CLUB RESORT

www.clubpollentia.com
On the outskirts of Port de Pollença, this large resort offers good accommodation in self-contained blocks and a broad range of activities, with cyclists arriving in the low season. Disadvantages: there's a big road outside and the beach is rocky.
⊞ H2 ⊠ Carretera Port de Pollença–Alcúdia km2 ☎ 971 546 996

PORTOFINO URBAN SEA HOTEL

www.urhotels.com
One of the crop of refurbished city-style hotels by the seaside to the east of Palma, the Portofino has minimalist décor. The pool is just metres from the promenade.
⊞ Off map at f5 (fold-out map)
⊠ Carrer Trafalgar, 24, Ciutat Jardí, Palma ☎ 971 260 464

SANTA CLARA HOTEL AND SPA

www.santaclarahotel.es
Blending a traditional building with modern minimalism, the Santa Clara follows the protocol for most new hotels in Palma, with a winning location, close to the cathedral, and a spa with steam room and sauna.
⊞ e4 ⊠ Carrer San Alonso, 16, Palma ☎ 971 729 231

Luxury Hotels

PRICES

Expect to pay upwards of €150 per night for a luxury hotel room.

ARABELLA SHERATON GOLF HOTEL SON VIDA

www.starwoodhotels.com
Golf is the main draw at Son Vida, with its own 18-hole course. But non-golfers can take tennis lessons or use the fitness facilities while children have their own pool and activities. Rooms are lavishly furnished and have their own balconies.

➕ D5 ✉ Carretera de la Vinagrella, Urbanización Son Vida, Palma ☎ 971 787 100

BELMOND LA RESIDENCIA

www.hotel-laresidencia.com
Formerly owned by Sir Richard Branson (still a regular visitor), Deià's most luxurious hotel is now managed by the Belmond luxury hotel group. Facilities include three restaurants, a bar, tennis courts, indoor and outdoor pools, a gym, steam room and spa. Rooms and suites vary in size, some with their own plunge pools or terraces.

➕ D4 ✉ Son Canals, Deià ☎ 971 636 046

CA'N AÍ

www.canai.com
Ca'n Aí delivers rural seclusion effortlessly, despite being on the edge of Sóller. Extensive gardens and citrus groves add to the peaceful ambience, while the 11 suites, often on a split level in the converted farmhouse, are rustic and untroubled by televisions.

➕ E3 ✉ Camí de Son Sales, 50, Sóller ☎ 971 632 494
◯ Closed Nov–end Feb

CONVENT DE LA MISSIÓ

www.conventdelamissio.com
Navigating this maze-like former church will take you past lounges decorated with modern art. The hotel's 14 minimalist bedrooms are decorated in cool creams and whites and are equally tranquil. But there is substance as well as style in this boutique hotel: the Simply Fosh restaurant (▷ 40) is highly regarded.

➕ e1 ✉ Carrer de la Missió, 7a, Palma ☎ 971 227 347

HOTEL GROUPS

Many major Spanish hotel groups have properties on Mallorca, including Barceló and Sol Meliá. Non-Spanish hotel groups include Sheraton, Relais & Chateaux and Belmond. However, 32 of Mallorca's leading independent hotels have joined together under the banner of Reis de Mallorca; these can be booked directly. For more information: www.reisdemallorca.com.

ILLA D'OR

www.hotelillador.com
The grande dame of Port de Pollença, the Illa d'Or has welcomed guests since 1929. It has a mainly British clientele, and a quiet, traditional atmosphere. Guests from the 119 rooms can eat at two restaurants or on the terrace right on the bay-front promenade. Facilities include a spa.

➕ H2 ✉ Passeig de Colón, 265, Port de Pollença ☎ 971 865 100 ◯ Closed late Nov–early Feb

READ'S HOTEL AND RESTAURANT

www.readshotel.com
Its outstanding spa, with a solarium and an ice room, has pushed Read's to the top of Mallorca's hotels. Boasting one of the island's best restaurants, the privately owned hotel also has a bistro and a cycling centre. The 23 rooms are individually decorated.

➕ F5 ✉ Carretera Santa Maria del Camí–Alaró, Santa Maria del Camí ☎ 971 140 261 ❓ No children under 14 years

SON BRULL

www.sonbrull.com
Stylish Son Brull has 23 tastefully minimalist rooms. Facilities include a spa, late-night bar and proximity to two golf clubs and Pollença town.

➕ H2 ✉ Carretera Palma–Pollença, Pollença ☎ 971 535 353 ◯ Closed Dec–Feb

Need to Know

Use this section to help you plan your visit to Mallorca. We have suggested the best ways to get around the island and useful information for when you are there.

Planning Ahead

When to Go

Summer is reliably hot and dry but spring and autumn can bring unpredictable weather. Winter can bring snow or balmy temperatures. The peak months of June to September are very busy so many people opt for May and October for smaller crowds and more reasonable temperatures.

TIME
L Mallorca is on CET (Central European Time), one hour ahead of GMT and six hours ahead of New York.

AVERAGE DAILY MAXIMUM TEMPERATURES

JAN	FEB	MAR	APR	MAY	JUN	JUL	AUG	SEP	OCT	NOV	DEC
57°F	59°F	63°F	66°F	72°F	79°F	84°F	84°F	81°F	73°F	64°F	59°F
14°C	15C	17°C	19°C	22°C	26°C	29°C	29°C	27°C	23°C	18°C	15°C

Spring This is the most changeable season; it can be very damp but you have a taste of summer without the oppressive heat. This is the season for cycling, walking and enjoying the blossom.

Summer With guaranteed sunshine you can expect wall-to-wall bodies on the beach during the summer school holidays. Prices are high, traffic slow and you might not be in the mood to do much more than flop by the pool.

Autumn Like spring, a wonderful time to visit, though bring waterproofs. The temperature of the sea remains warm but the crowds have gone.

Winter The resorts might close for winter but this is still a good time for a city break in Palma, where there is plenty going on. Pack walking boots and take your chances in the hills.

WHAT'S ON

January *Cabalgata de los Reyes Magos* (5 Jan): The Three Kings arrive by boat in Palma with gifts for the city's children.

Sant Antoni Abat (16–17 Jan): Processions of pets and farm animals in Palma, Artà and Sa Pobla.

Sant Sebastià (19–20 Jan): Bonfires and barbecues in Palma's squares.

February *Sa Rúa* (last weekend before Lent): Carnival held in Palma and elsewhere with bonfires, fancy dress and processions.

March/April *Semana Santa* (Holy Week): Processions and celebrations in Palma and elsewhere on the island.

May *Moros I Cristians* (8–10 May): Mock battles in Sóller, commemorating a 1561 battle.

June *Sant Pere* (28–29 Jun): Processions of fishing boats in Palma, Port d'Andratx and Port d'Alcúdia.

July *La Virgen del Carmen* (16 Jul): Processions of boats in the island's ports.

Santa Catalina Thomas (27–28 Jul): Homage to Mallorca's patron saint in her home town of Valldemossa.

August *Sant Bartomeu* (24 Aug): Devil-dancing in Montuiri at one of Mallorca's oldest festivals.

Sant Agustí (28 Aug): Cavallets dances in Felanitx, with children dressed as horses being chased by giants.

September Harvest festival including a wine festival in Binissalem (last Sun in Sep) and a melon festival in Vilafranca de Bonany (second Sun in Sep).

December *Festa de l'Estendard* (31 Dec): Palma commemorates the anniversary of the Christian conquest.

Mallorca Online

www.spain.info
Official website of the Spanish Tourism Office with useful information, although not as detailed as the websites of the regional offices.

www.illesbalears.es
Website of the tourism department for the Balearic Islands and a very helpful resource with plenty of factual information. Good events section and the beach search facility allows you to find clean, safe beaches. Has links to the accommodation search facility of Mallorca's Hotel Federation.

www.mallorca-beaches.com
A comprehensive guide to the island's beaches, with descriptions, plus information on water-parks, other tourist-geared activities and a hotel booking service.

www.mallorcahotelguide.com
Official accommodation search engine for Mallorca.

www.infomallorca.net
Tourism website of the local government with lots of information on sport, culture and transport (including timetables to download) as well as an accommodation search facility.

www.vamos-mallorca.com
Month-by-month events guide to be downloaded for free; the online version of a magazine available in tourist offices.

www.reisdemallorca.com
An organization of 32 or so independent hotels around the island with links direct to the hotels.

www.rusticbooking.com
An accommodation search facility for the island's rural *fincas* and small hotels. Clear and easy to use.

INTERNET ACCESS

Many hotels on Mallorca offer WiFi. Some charge for usage and rates can be expensive. Few cafés offer internet access. Better restaurants, bars and cafés also offer WiFi, as well as larger shopping centres.

ONLINE BOOKINGS

Your holiday on Mallorca can be booked at your laptop: flights, hotels, cars and even some activities can be booked online before you leave your house. But how can you get the best price? Timing is critical. Popular periods will be booked long in advance so start planning as soon as possible. But if you're aiming to visit out of the high season, you can expect some discounts. Price comparison websites can help you find the best deal—though you will need to book with a credit card.

USEFUL TRAVEL SITE

www.fodors.com
A complete travel-planning site. You can research prices and weather; book air tickets, cars and rooms; pose questions to fellow travellers; and find links to other sites.

Getting There

VISAS AND PASSPORTS

● All visitors must have a valid passport (or an EU national ID card).

● EU visitors do not require a visa, but for stays longer than three months you must register in person at the Oficina de Extrajeros (Foreigners' Office).

● Visitors from many countries require a visa if staying longer than 90 days. Check with your consul before departure.

● Passengers on all flights to and from Spain are required to supply advance passenger information (API) to the Spanish authorities—full names, nationality, date of birth and travel document details, namely a passport number. This information is compulsory. Travel agents can collect this information at the time of booking, or give it to staff at check-in desks. Online give the information at the time of booking.

HEALTH AND INSURANCE

● Travel insurance is strongly advised.

● EU nationals can use a European Health Insurance Card (EHIC) for free emergency health care.

● Dental treatment is not covered by the EU's reciprocal health agreements.

AIRPORT

Palma's Son Sant Joan airport (tel: 902 404 704; www.aena.es) is 8km (5 miles) east of the city and is well connected by road. The airport is one of the busiest in Europe and receives flights from all over the world, especially from northern Europe in the summer. There are all the facilities of a major airport, including currency exchanges, banks, tourist information and shops.

GETTING TO AND FROM THE AIRPORT

Until the need for an airport rail shuttle is agreed, the only way to reach Palma from the airport is by road. A taxi rank operates 24 hours a day and the 8km (5-mile) drive into the city takes approximately 20 minutes, depending on the time of day. Journeys will be metered and typically cost about €25 to central Palma. The number one bus runs every 15 minutes from 6am to 2am from a stop between the taxi rank and the multi-storey car park. It stops at the Plaça d'Espanya, a hub for bus services around the city (▷ 118) and a useful point for onward travel. Many hotels will arrange collection by coach from the airport or you can rent a car from all the major firms in the airport.

PORTS

Mallorca is linked to mainland Spain (Valencia, Barcelona) and the other Balearic islands (Menorca, Ibiza) by various ferry services to Palma and Port d'Alcúdia. Cars and motorbikes are carried by some of the ferries but the overnight passage is expensive.

CONSULATES

● UK
✉ Convent dels Caputxins, 4, Edificio Orisba B, 4ºD, Palma
☎ 971 717 520

● US
✉ Carrer Porto Pí, 8, Palma
☎ 971 403 707

● Germany
✉ Carrer Porto Pí, 8, Palma
☎ 971 707 737

CAR RENTAL

If you intend to see more of the island than your hotel's vicinity, a rental car is the best option. Rates are competitive and there are several reliable local companies, which offer a drop-off and collection service, as well as the major international brands, all of which have desks at Palma airport.

TAXIS

Official taxis are abundant in Palma; they're usually cream in colour. All journeys will be metered; rates rise at night and weekends. Taxi ranks are located throughout Palma, including the airport: there's a small surcharge for trips to and from the airport. Outside Palma, taxi liveries are more varied but again all taxis will be metered.

CAR RENTAL AGENCIES

The following companies have agencies in the arrivals hall at Palma's airport:

● Avis
☎ 971 789 187
www.avis-europe.com

● Goldcar
☎ 965 943 186
www.goldcar.es

● Hertz
☎ 971 789 670
www.hertz.com

● Sixt
☎ 902 491 616
www.sixt.com

Getting Around

BUSES

Palma and its surrounding bay has a very good bus service with its own company covering routes in the city (Empresa Municipal de Transportes, or EMT: ☎ 971 214 444 or 900 700 710; www.emtpalma.es). The hub for services around the city is the bus station at Plaça d'Espanya. There are also good bus links between Mallorca's towns and resorts operated by Transport de les Illes Balears, or TIB (☎ 971 177 777; www.tib.org), although services are less frequent and may cease completely in the winter months. Tickets are available as single or return.

SIGHTSEEING BUS

The City Sightseeing bus (www.city-sightseeing. com) provides a good overview of Palma's principal sights. Fares cost from €15 and the full round-trip takes 80 minutes. The bus serves certain outlying areas of the city, such as Castell de Bellver to the west, and is a useful addition to the EMT bus network. You can hop onto the bus at any of its 16 stops: there is one just opposite the cathedral.

DRIVING

Driving on Mallorca is on the right and at roundabouts you must give way to traffic from the left. A smaller car is recommended as many of the streets in the towns and villages are extremely narrow. Driving offences are taken very seriously by the Spanish police; these include using a mobile phone while driving, speeding and drink-driving. Roads on Mallorca are generally good—a motorway from Palma past Llucmajor gives speedy access to the east coast and the Ma-13 road from Palma to Alcúdia is a dual carriageway. Roads in the Serra de Tramuntana can be narrow, congested and precipitous. There are plenty of fuel stops around the island. Parking in towns can be difficult, particularly during the peak season of June to September, but pay-and-display car parks are usually clearly signposted.

TRAINS AND TRAMS

Most train services on Mallorca are of more use to local workers than sightseers, with one exception: the Palma–Sóller line via Bunyola (www.trendesoller.com). Old-fashioned carriages and beautiful scenery are two reasons to take the train at least once. In Sóller you can continue your journey to Port de Sóller by tram. Mallorca's other train routes are from Palma to Sa Pobla and Manacor, both via Marratxi and Inca.

PALMA'S METRO

Palma's metro opened in 2007 and comprises two lines. Line M1 runs from the Plaça d'Espanya to the University campus via nine stops, while line M2 runs along the main train line and serves seven stations before terminating at the city suburb of Marratxi. Neither line is of particular use to tourists.

BOAT

Boat tours operate from several ports around the island. The most popular are tours to Sa Dragonera and Illa de Cabrera (▷ 98). Ferries connect Port d'Alcúdia to Menorca and Palma to Ibiza and mainland Spain.

SCOOTER, BICYCLE AND MOTORCYCLE

Scooters and bicycles are popular ways of getting around towns and resorts and can be rented from companies in the town. Tour operators also offer motorcycle tours of the island for qualified riders. It is compulsory to wear a helmet when riding a scooter or motorcycle; rental companies often include helmets in the price. Insurance is also often included in the rental agreement; never decline it. You will also need a valid driving licence to rent a scooter. Some tips for safe scooter riding: watch out for people opening car doors into the street; avoid riding along the inside of traffic when there is a right turn ahead; don't carry a passenger unless the scooter is designed for two and the other person has a helmet.

PUBLIC HOLIDAYS

1 Jan: New Year's Day
6 Jan: Epiphany
Mar/Apr: Maundy Thursday
Mar/Apr: Good Friday
Mar/Apr: Easter Monday
1 May: Labour Day
15 Aug: Assumption of the Virgin
12 Oct: National Day
1 Nov: All Saint's Day
6 Dec: Constitution Day
8 Dec: Immaculate Conception
25 Dec: Christmas Day
26 Dec: St. Stephen's Day

VISITORS WITH DISABILITIES

Mallorca has made great efforts to be more wheelchair friendly. More recent attractions—such as Palma's aquarium—have full wheelchair access. The capital's buses are all accessible to wheelchair users. Older sights and hotels are being gradually updated and in some of the resorts (Palma Nova, Magaluf, Illetes, Santa Ponça and Peguera) amphibious wheelchairs are available for disabled swimmers.

Essential Facts

ELECTRICITY

● Voltage is 220 volts and sockets take two round pins.

MONEY

The euro is the currency of Mallorca. Banknotes are in denominations of €5, €10, €20, €50, €100, €200 and €500. Coins are in denominations of 1, 2, 5, 10, 20 and 50 cents and €1 and €2. Credit cards are widely accepted. Smaller shops and market stalls may prefer cash. Banks will change money and traveller's cheques, and ATMs (known as *telebancos*) dispense cash. Your bank may charge you for using your credit or debit card to withdraw money from an ATM.

EMERGENCY NUMBERS

All emergencies: 112
Ambulances: 061
Municipal Police: 092
National Police: 091
Fire Service: 085
Coastguard: 900 202 202

LOST PROPERTY

● Palma airport has a lost property office (☎ 971 789 456) but if the item was lost while on the plane it is likely to have been returned to your airline's own lost property office; it is a good idea to check both.

MEASUREMENTS

● Mallorca uses the metric system. Distances are measured in metres and kilometres, fuel is sold by the litre and food is weighed in grams and kilograms.
● Clothing and footwear sizes use the European metric scale.

MOBILE TELEPHONES

● Check with your mobile phone operator that your tariff and phone will work abroad and remember that you will be charged for receiving as well as making calls.
● Call charges are higher than at home; buying a pay-as-you-go SIM card from a Spanish operator in Mallorca will reduce charges if you plan to use your phone a lot.
● Mobile coverage is good across much of the island although in rural areas the signal may be weak.

POST

● Post boxes from the Spanish post office (*Correos*) are yellow and are widespread.
● Stamps are called *segells* and are readily available.
● Spanish addresses may abbreviate Carrer to c/. *Sin número (s/n)* means without number: usually a junction or corner.

TELEPHONES

● All telephone numbers in Spain have nine digits. The regional code for Mallorca is 971, which must be included even when making a local call.

● Public telephone booths are blue and can be used with coins and cards. Remember that using a hotel telephone can be expensive.

● International dialling codes include:
UK: 00 44
USA: 00 1
Ireland: 00 353
Australia: 00 61
Germany: 00 49
Netherlands: 00 31
Mainland Spain: 00 34

TELEVISION

● Most hotels have news channels in several languages (typically English, French and German).

● The main Spanish television channels are TVE1, TVE2 and, in Catalan, TVE3.

TOILETS

● Although Palma has one of the world's most advanced waste disposal systems (rubbish is whizzed along underground), public lavatories *(lavabos)* are much harder to find.

● Department stores and museums will have public lavatories or you can try restaurants and cafés.

TOURIST INFORMATION OFFICES

● Palma
✉ Plaça de la Reina, 2
☎ 971 173 990

✉ Aeropuerto
☎ 971 789 556

● Cala d'Or
✉ Perico Pomar, 10
☎ 971 657 463

● Cala Millor
✉ Avenida Joan Servera Camps, Son Servera
☎ 971 585 864

● Cala Sant Vicenç
✉ Plaça Cala Sant Vicenç
☎ 971 533 264

● Magaluf
✉ Pere Vaquer Ramis, 1
☎ 971 131 126

● Port d'Alcúdia
✉ Passeig Marítim
☎ 971 547 257

● Port de Pollença
✉ Monges, 9
☎ 971 865 467

● Sóller
✉ Plaça d'Espanya
☎ 971 638 008

● Valldemossa
✉ Avinguda de Palma, 7
☎ 971 612 019

NEED TO KNOW ESSENTIAL FACTS

Language

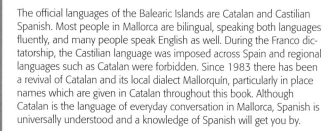

The official languages of the Balearic Islands are Catalan and Castilian Spanish. Most people in Mallorca are bilingual, speaking both languages fluently, and many people speak English as well. During the Franco dictatorship, the Castilian language was imposed across Spain and regional languages such as Catalan were forbidden. Since 1983 there has been a revival of Catalan and its local dialect Mallorquín, particularly in place names which are given in Catalan throughout this book. Although Catalan is the language of everyday conversation in Mallorca, Spanish is universally understood and a knowledge of Spanish will get you by.

Spanish

BASIC VOCABULARY	
good morning	buenos dias
good afternoon/ evening	buenas tardes
good night	buenas noches
hello (informal)	hola
goodbye (informal)	hasta luego/hasta pronto
hello (on the phone)	¿Diga?
goodbye	adios
please	por favor
thank you	gracias
you're welcome	de nada
how are you? (formal)	¿Cómo está?
how are you? (informal)	¿Que tal?
I'm fine	estoy bien
I'm sorry	lo siento
excuse me	perdón
I don't understand	no entiendo
I don't speak Spanish	no hablo español
how much is it?	¿cuanto es?
where is the…?	¿dónde está…?
do you have…?	¿tiene…?
I'd like…	me gustaría
I don't know	No lo sé
It doesn't matter	No importa
How much/many?	¿Cuánto/cuántos?
Is/are there?	¿Hay?

USEFUL WORDS	
yes	sí
no	no
Where?	¿Dónde?
When?	¿Cuándo?
Why?	¿Por qué?
What?	¿Que?
Who?	¿Quién?
How?	¿Cómo?
ticket	entrada
big	grande
small	pequeño
with	con
without	sin
hot	caliente
cold	frío
early	temprano
late	tarde
here	aquí
there	alli
today	hoy
tomorrow	mañana
yesterday	ayer
menu	la carta
entrance	entrada
exit	salida
open	abierto
closed	cerrado
good	bueno
bad	malo

Catalan

BASIC VOCABULARY

yes/no	si/no
please	per favor
thank you	gràcies
welcome	de res
hello	hola
goodbye	adéu
good morning	bon dia
good afternoon	bona tarda
goodnight	bona nit
excuse me	perdoni
you're welcome	de res
how are you?	com va?
do you speak English?	parla anglès?
I don't understand	no ho entenc
today	avui
tomorrow	demà

MONEY

how much?	quant es?
bank	banc
exchange office	oficina de canvi
coin	moneda
change	camvi
banknote	bitllet de banc
cheque	xec
traveller's cheque	xec de viatge
credit card	carta de crèdit
exchange rate	tant per cent
commission charge	comissió

TRANSPORTATION

how do I get to…?	per anar a…?
single ticket	senzill-a
return ticket	anar i tornar
aeroplane/airport	avió/aeroport
train	tren
bus	autobús
car	cotxe

HOTELS

hotel	hotel
bed and breakfast	llit i berenar
single room	habitació senzilla
double room	habitació doble
one person	una persona
one night	una nit
reservation	reservas
room service	servei d'habitació
bath	bany
shower	dutxa
toilet	toaleta
key	clau
lift	ascensor
balcony	balcó
sea view	vista al mar

EATING OUT

open	obert
closed	tancat
café	cafè
pub/bar	celler
breakfast	berenar
lunch	dinar
dinner	sopar
waiter	cambrer
waitress	cambrera
starter	primer plat
main course	segón plat
dessert	postres
bill	cuenta
beer	cervesa
wine	vi
water	aigua

Timeline

ROMANS

The all-conquering Romans brought vines and olive trees from Italy to make their new colony more comfortable. They also built roads, aqueducts and bridges—the most famous example is Pont Romà near Pollença, although few original features remain. But the Roman capital on the island, Pollentia (now Alcúdia, ▷ 80–81) retains several Roman constructions.

From left to right: Capocorb Vell Talaiotic site; Roman city of Pollentia near Alcúdia; the pilgrim's route to Castell d'Alaró; interior of La Seu; a bronze statue of Fra Junípero Serra in Palma; the marble belvedere in the grounds of Son Marroig

5000 BC Mallorca's first inhabitants arrive by boat, probably from the Iberian Peninsula.

1400–800 BC The Talaiotic era brings the island's first organized settlements, ruins of which remain today at Àrta and Capocorb Vell.

123 BC Roman consul Quintus Caecilius Metellus leads a successful Roman invasion of Mallorca, starting settlements at Pollentia (Alcúdia) and Palmeria (Palma).

AD 425 The Vandals invade Mallorca, driving out the Romans who leave vineyards and olive groves.

AD 902 The Moors conquer Mallorca bringing the island under the control of the Emirate of Córdoba for three centuries.

1229 King Jaume I of Aragón captures Palma and the island becomes part of the Catalan monarchy.

1311–1349 The kingdom passes through several pairs of hands until the Battle of Llucmajor when Jaume III is killed and the kingdom of Mallorca ends.

1479 King Fernando V of Aragón marries Isabel I of Castile, paving the way for modern, unified Spain but Mallorca is left out.

1715 Mallorca is the last province to surrender to the victorious King Felipe V in the War of

Spanish Succession and has Castilian imposed over the Catalan language as punishment.

1749 Father Junípero Serra, a priest from Petra, sets off for the New World, founding missions in Mexico and California that become San Francisco and other cities.

1875 The railway line from Palma to Inca opens. Mallorca begins to thrive on trade and wealthy merchants build lavish mansions.

1903 The Gran Hotel Sóller is built; entrepreneur Thomas Cook offers tours of Mallorca.

1915 Austrian Archduke Ludwig Salvador, ecologist, philanthropist and womanizer, dies, having bought up much of the land between Valldemossa and Deiá.

1936 General Francisco Franco leads a military rebellion, causing three years of civil war.

1975 Death of General Franco; Mallorca emerges from decades of repressive rule.

1983 The Balearic Islands gain regional autonomy.

2002 Introduction of the euro.

2011 The Serra de Tramuntana is registered as a UNESCO world heritage site.

PIRATES

When Mallorca's influence had waned after the island's kingdom disintegrated, it became subject to pirate attacks. During the 16th century watchtowers were built around the coastline to provide early warning of pirates. The most notorious pirate rampage occurred in 1561 when a band of Turkish pirates was vanquished by Sóller's women—an event that is commemorated in early May each year.

TOURIST INVASION

As a Mediterranean island, Mallorca has seen invaders come and go for many millennia. But in the 1920s author Gordon West presaged the 20th-century invasion of Mallorca in his book *Jogging Round Mallorca*. The invaders? Sunseeking tourists. In this new century, Mallorca is still surviving the annual onslaught of tourists and reaping the rewards.

Index

INDEX

TwinPack Mallorca

Published by AA Publishing, a trading name of AA Media Limited, whose registered office is Fanum House, Basing View, Basingstoke, Hampshire RG21 4EA. Registered number 06112600.

© **AA Media Limited 2015**
First published 2000
New edition 2015

Written by Robin Barton
Updated by Josephine Quintero
Series editor Clare Ashton
Cover design Tracey Freestone, Nick Johnston
Design work Tracey Freestone
Image retouching and repro Ian Little

Colour separation by AA Digital Department
Printed and bound by Leo Paper Products, China

A CIP catalogue record for this book is available from the British Library.

ISBN 978-0-7495-7675-2

A05274
Maps in this title produced from mapping © MAIRDUMONT / Falk Verlag 2014

The Automobile Association would like to thank the following photographers, companies and picture libraries for their assistance in the preparation of this book.

Abbreviations for the pictures credits are as follows – (t) top; (b) bottom; (c) centre; (l) left; (r) right; (AA) AA World Travel Library.

2–18 top panel AA/K Paterson; **4** AA/C Sawyer; **5** AA/K Paterson; **6tl** AA/C Sawyer; **6tc** AA/K Paterson; **6tr** AA/K Paterson; **6bl** AA/P Baker; **6bc(i)** AA/C Sawyer; **6bc(ii)** AA/M Chaplow; **6br** AA/C Sawyer; **7tl** AA/K Paterson; **7tc** AA/K Paterson; **7tr** AA/K Paterson; **7bl** AA/K Paterson; **7bc** AA/K Paterson; **7br** AA/C Sawyer; **10t** AA/C Sawyer; **10c(i)** AA/K Paterson; **10c(ii)** AA/C Sawyer; **10b** AA/C Sawyer; **11t(i)** AA/K Paterson; **11t(ii)** AA/P Baker; **11c(i)** AA/C Sawyer; **11c(ii)** AA/K Paterson; **11b** AA/K Paterson; **12t** AA/C Sawyer; **12c(i)** AA/K Paterson; **12c(ii)** AA/C Sawyer; **12b** AA/J Cowham; **13t(i)** AA/K Paterson; **13t(ii)** AA/K Paterson; **13c(i)** AA/S Day; **13c(ii)** Digitalvision; **13b** AA/K Paterson; **14t** AA/E Meacher; **14c(i)** AA/M Chaplow; **14c(ii)** AA/C Sawyer; **14b** AA/K Paterson; **15** AA/C Sawyer; **16t** AA/C Sawyer; **16c(i)** AA/K Paterson; **16c(ii)** AA/K Paterson; **16b** AA/P Baker; **17t** AA/P Baker; **17c(i)** AA/C Sawyer; **17c(ii)** AA/J Cowham; **17b** AA/C Sawyer; **18t** AA/P Baker; **18c(i)** AA/P Baker; **18c(ii)** AA/J Cowham; **18b** AA/P Baker; **19t(i)** AA/P Baker; **19t(ii)** AA/K Paterson; **19c** AA/P Baker; **19b(i)** AA/P Baker; **19b(ii)** AA/K Paterson; **20/21** AA/J Cowham; **24l** AA/K Paterson; **24r** AA/C Sawyer; **25l** AA/C Sawyer; **25c** AA/K Paterson; **25r** AA/K Paterson; **26l** AA/P Baker; **26c** AA/P Baker; **26r** AA/K Paterson; **27** AA/P Baker; **28l** AA/C Sawyer; **28r** AA/K Paterson; **29l** Courtesy of Palma Acuarium, Palma de Mallorca; **29r** Courtesy of Palma Acuarium, Palma de Mallorca; **30l** AA/K Paterson; **30t** AA/K Paterson; **30/31b** AA/C Sawyer; **31t** AA/K Paterson; **31bl** AA/K Paterson; **31br** AA/K Paterson; **32–35** top panel AA/K Paterson; **32l** AA/P Baker; **32r** AA/K Paterson; **33l** AA/C Sawyer; **33r** AA/C Sawyer; **34l** AA/P Baker; **34r** AA/C Sawyer; **35l** AA/J Cowham; **35r** AA/P Baker; **36** AA/C Sawyer; **37** AA/K Paterson; **38** AA/K Paterson; **39–40** AA/C Sawyer; **41** AA/K Paterson; **44l** AA/P Baker; **44r** © Successió Miró/ADAGP, Paris and DACS, London 2009; **45l** AA/K Paterson; **45c** AA/P Baker; **45r** AA/P Baker; **46l** AA/J Cowham; **46tr** AA/K Paterson; **46br** AA/K Paterson; **47t** AA/K Paterson; **47bl** AA/K Paterson; **47br** AA/K Paterson; **48–49** top panel AA/P Baker; **48l** AA/C Sawyer; **48r** AA/P Baker; **49l** AA/K Paterson; **49r** AA/K Paterson; **50** AA/K Paterson; **51** AA/K Paterson; **52** AA/C Sawyer; **53** AA/P Baker; **56l** AA/P Baker; **56r** AA/K Paterson; **57** AA/K Paterson; **58l** AA/P Baker; **58r** AA/K Paterson; **59** AA/K Paterson; **60** AA/K Paterson; **61t** AA/K Paterson; **61bl** AA/C Sawyer; **61br** AA/K Paterson; **62l** AA/J Cowham; **62r** AA/K Paterson; **63t** AA/P Baker; **63br** AA/C Sawyer; **63bl** AA/P Baker; **64l** AA/P Baker; **64tr** AA/C Sawyer; **64br** AA/K Paterson; **65t** AA/K Paterson; **65bl** AA/P Baker; **65br** AA/K Paterson; **66** AA/C Sawyer; **67t** AA/C Sawyer; **67bl** AA/K Paterson; **67br** AA/K Paterson; **68t** AA/W Voysey; **68bl** AA/K Paterson; **68br** AA/K Paterson; **69tl** AA/K Paterson; **69bl** AA/K Paterson; **69r** AA/W Voysey; **70–71** top panel AA/K Paterson; **70l** AA/J Cowham; **70r** AA/K Paterson; **71l** AA/C Sawyer; **71r** AA/K Paterson; **72** AA/P Baker; **73** AA/K Paterson; **74** AA/K Paterson; **75** AA/K Paterson; **76** AA/C Sawyer; **77** AA/K Paterson; **80l** AA/P Baker; **80/81tc** AA/C Sawyer; **80/81bc** AA/P Baker; **81r** AA/C Sawyer; **82l** Courtesy of the Fundación Yannick y Ben Jakober; **82c** Courtesy of the Fundación Yannick y Ben Jakober; **82r** Courtesy of the Fundación Yannick y Ben Jakober; **83** Courtesy of the Fundación Yannick y Ben Jakober; **84l** AA/P Baker; **84c** AA/P Baker; **84r** AA/K Paterson; **85l** AA/C Sawyer; **85r** AA/P Baker; **86–87** top panel AA/P Baker; **86l** AA/K Paterson; **86r** AA/K Paterson; **87l** AA/C Sawyer; **87r** AA/P Baker; **88** AA/K Paterson; **89** AA/K Paterson; **90** AA/C Sawyer; **91** AA/P Baker; **94l** AA/P Baker; **94r** AA/K Paterson; **95** AA/P Baker; **96** AA/K Paterson; **97l** Courtesy of Cuevas del Drach Mallorca; **97tr** Courtesy of Cuevas del Drach Mallorca; **97br** Courtesy of Cuevas del Drach Mallorca; **98l** AA/C Sawyer; **98r** AA/C Sawyer; **99l** AA/C Sawyer; **99c** AA/K Paterson; **99r** AA/J Cowham; **100l** AA/C Sawyer; **100c** AA/C Sawyer; **100r** AA/C Sawyer; **101–103** top panel AA/P Baker; **101l** AA/K Paterson; **101r** AA/J Cowham; **102l** AA/H Rainbow; **102r** AA/K Paterson; **103l** AA/K Paterson; **103r** AA/K Paterson; **104** AA/K Paterson; **105t** AA/K Paterson; **105b** AA/K Paterson; **106** AA/C Sawyer; **107** AA/C Sawyer; **108–109** top panel AA/C Sawyer; **108t** AA/C Sawyer; **108c(i)** AA/C Sawyer; **108c(ii)** AA/C Sawyer; **108b** AA/C Sawyer; **113** AA/K Paterson; **114–125** top panel AA/P Baker; **124l** AA/C Sawyer; **124c** AA/P Baker; **124r** AA/P Baker; **125l** AA/K Paterson; **125c** AA/P Baker; **125r** AA/K Paterson.

Every effort has been made to trace the copyright holders, and we apologise in advance for any accidental errors. We would be happy to apply any corrections in the following edition of this publication.